Seeing

Simon Turley: It has taken me a long time to pupate/mutate from being a teacher who writes to a writer who teaches.

I have lived in Plymouth for more than twenty years. I have worked with some theatre companies: Barbican Theatre, Theatre Royal Plymouth and its Young Company, the Trevenna Company, Paines Plough, Girls' Own. I am working with BBC TV – *Doctors* and *Breakers*.

Seeing Without Light

Simon Turley

DRUM THEATRE PLYMOUTH
www.theatreroyal.com

PARTHIAN

Parthian
The Old Surgery
Napier Street
Cardigan
SA43 1ED

www.parthianbooks.co.uk

First published in 2005
© Simon Turley 2005
All Rights Reserved

ISBN 1-902638-63-8

Cover design by Steve John/Dragonfly Design
Printed and bound by Dinefwr Press, Llandybïe, Wales
Typeset by type@lloydrobson.com & Parthian

Parthian is an independent publisher which works with the support of the Arts Council of Wales and the Welsh Books Council

British Library Cataloguing in Publication Data – A cataloguing record for this book is available from the British Library

This book is sold subject to the condition that it shall not by way of trade or otherwise be circulated without the publisher's prior consent in any form of binding or cover other than that in which it is published and without a similar condition including the condition being imposed on the subsequent purchaser

Theatre of Science

The Theatre Royal Plymouth's *Theatre of Science* promises to be an exciting new initiative for Plymouth and the wider region, bringing theatre and science together in innovative and creative ways. It also hopes to create a lasting legacy of science-based plays for British theatre in general.

Key elements of the year-long project will be three specially-commissioned theatre productions; scientists-in-residence working alongside theatre practitioners; an exciting new science drama programme for local schools and partner community groups; and an intensive programme of public projects and events. Participants of all ages and abilities will have the opportunity to be involved.

Particular issues to be addressed include biomedical science and the ethical and moral issues behind disease immunity, eugenics, the ageing process and contemporary genomics. This unique project will explore the potential for performance arts not only to promote an understanding of contemporary biomedical science, but also to establish a dialogue between the often conflicting cultures of theatre and science.

Theatre of Science has three aims:

- to research, test and evaluate innovative ways of bringing dramatists and scientists together to shape medical-linked theatre, community and education projects;

- to use the performing arts to address the major scientific, ethical and moral problems and opportunities of biomedicine in the 21st century;

- to enable creative science partnerships which inspire and develop new audiences and future practitioners for both science and theatre.

Theatre of Science will present three specially-commissioned productions – two in the Drum Theatre and one at TR2. Each production will have an extensive education programme for local schools.

The first *Theatre of Science* production is *Seeing Without Light* by Simon Turley (Drum Theatre, Thursday 27 January – Saturday 5 February 2005). This play was originally developed in association with Dr Jane McHarg, Research Fellow at the Peninsula Medical School, and Dr Penny Fiddler from @ Bristol, then by Professor Anthony Pinching, Associate Dean for Cornwall at the Peninsula Medical School. The play explores the ramifications of the discovery of genetic immunity to HIV; attitudes to the disease in its African context; and the similar responsibilities of scientists and artists to their work. This is a contemporary drama that questions universal themes of love, life and death in the 21st century, while exploring how life, art and science imitate one another. The Eddystone Trust in Plymouth is the community partner for this play and ten local schools will work with science and theatre practitioners in workshops exploring the biomedical and ethical issues of HIV research and treatment. They will present their own plays at TR2 in January 2005, before the first production of *Seeing Without Light*.

The second play is *Still Life* by Charles Way (Drum Theatre, Thu 14 - Sat 23 April 2005). This play explores the link between DNA and longevity and the ethics of genetic research and how science is challenging not only our moral universe but what it is that makes us human. Professor John McLachlan, Professor of Medical Education at the Peninsula Medical School, will support this production and will be scientific advisor across the wider *Theatre of Science* project.

Special by Peter Morgan completes the trilogy of plays and explores the medical and cultural history of eugenics and its contemporary resonances with modern genomics. This play benefited from a Wellcome-funded script development week at the Theatre Royal in 2003 and subsequent research at the Wellcome Library. The play received its first reading at RADA in April 2004 and a second in Sweden over the summer, as part of a Wellcome Trust initiative.

The *Theatre of Science*'s SciArt laboratory will offer a chance for artists, locally and all over the country, to work in collaboration with scientists on new ideas. The SciArt lab will offer a series of commissions to explore the links between art and science.

Rebecca Gould, Associate Director at Theatre Royal Plymouth, has worked closely with Professor John McLachlan from the Peninsula Medical School on *Theatre of Science* and the project has been generously funded by a grant from the Wellcome Trust and forms part of a collaborative programme with Creative Partnerships.

Seeing Without Light

First performed at the Drum Theatre Plymouth
31 January 2005.

Cast:

Hawa	–	Krissi Bohn
Paul	–	Jonathan Lisle
Dan	–	John Morrisey
Rachel	–	Clare Wille

Creative Team:

Director	–	Jeff Teare
Designer	–	Jane Linz Roberts
Video Designer	–	Thomas Hall
Lighting Designer	–	Bruno Poet
Sound Designer	–	Richard Price
Scientific Advisor	–	Professor Anthony Pinching
Producer	–	Rebecca Gould
Production Manager	–	Nick Soper
Stage Manager	–	Sue Berry
Deputy Stage Manager	–	Sally Coleman
Wardrobe Supervisor	–	Dina Hall
Wardrobe Mistress	–	Cheryl Hill
Drum Technician	–	Symon Harner
Press	–	Cameron Duncan (01386 700456)

Set, props and costumes made by
TR2 – Theatre Royal Production and Education Centre

A flexible space, able to contain up to three acting areas simultaneously and represent many locations. A screen.

Scene 1

Actor/Screen: One time.

Rich yellow light on a stone pestle and mortar. HAWA enters the light with a small sack of grain – millet ready to be ground. She measures a bowlful into the mortar and pauses, pestle in hand. She focuses off.

Hawa (*softly, smiling*): Kito... sleep little man....

Slowly she turns back to the mortar. Still smiling, she starts to work it with the pestle. A practised action. She pitches her words over her shoulder, off.

Hawa: Kito.

Silence.

Hawa: I called you Kito... precious. Precious one.

Silence.

Hawa: When you were born your grandmother said 'Guedado', I said 'Kito' back. Precious.

HAWA hums as she continues to work the grain. White light on DAN. He sits on a wooden chair, holding a bottle of mineral water. There is a careful arrangement of kitchen equipment beside him: copper pans, utensils; professional gear. He has a script that lies open on the floor at his feet. There is a camera on a tripod.

Dan (*a rehearsal*): He'd cook. He was a brilliant cook. And I miss that. I miss that, certainly. We'd have people round. And I'd lose him for the afternoon. I wasn't really allowed in the kitchen.

Light slowly up on a bed, where PAUL and RACHEL lie in one another's arms. The screen above them shows the ennucleation process – micropipette breaking cell wall of the ovum.

Dan: I made the mistake of offering, to start with... you know, just to do the skivvying, and that. And he let me... but every vegetable I peeled or chopped, I saw he'd kind of be trimming again, or altering the angle, for fuck's sake, of the slices I'd made....

Paul (*softly*): Did you say something?

Dan: Drove me mad.

Paul: Rachel?

DAN unscrews the lid of the mineral water and takes a sip. He replaces the lid. He leafs through the script on the floor.

Hawa: When you are awake, you cough and I want that you should sleep. When you sleep I have to tie my hands and feet together to stop myself from nudging you back to be awake again.

HAWA works the grain.

Dan: Then I realised I was taking the joy out of it – helping. So I just got on with something else. And I'd listen to him, down in here, making every pan ring – with the gas roaring up around them. I was jealous – of the pans... getting all that vigorous attention.

DAN rereads the script silently, editing it. HAWA continues to work the grain.

Paul: Rachel.

Rachel: What?

Paul: Say something. *Any*thing... say anything.

Rachel (*nonplussed*): I love you?

Paul (*playful*): That would do... short of, I dunno, 'You're a great shag, you animal', or, 'Every moment we spend together is a voyage of discovery.'

Rachel: No one says stuff like that.

Paul: Or, whatever.... I'm thinking of painting a view of us fucking on the ceiling.

Rachel: Why would I think that? *I* can't draw.

Paul: Not you, *me*. I'd paint that – us – up there on the ceiling of the Pristine Chapel. I *mean* it. I was just thinking that would be really beautiful. *I* was thinking of doing that... then... just then... what were *you* thinking just then while I was thinking that? Tell me....

Rachel: Painting? When did you ever start a painting? You don't do paint... it would be photography... wouldn't it... and that would, basically, be porn, or something.

Paul (*sharp*): That's what you're thinking *now*. I asked you what were you thinking *then*.

RACHEL breaks away from PAUL. He watches her – hurt.

Rachel: Sorry.

Paul: What's wrong?

Rachel: I'm sorry, okay?

Dan (*of the kitchen gear*): Nobody uses this lot now. They've been hanging, useless, on the rack we bought, so he could sort of just look up and unhook one at a critical moment and slam it down on the flames, throw stuff in it and let it take whatever colour and flavour and texture he wanted... he'd like shake it and it would ignite for a moment... or he'd lean tight down over it and stir it so delicately.

Paul: Hey. You have a freckle that I love.

Rachel: I've got millions of them.

Paul: I'm just starting to appreciate this particular one. Freckle One.

Dan: Our kitchen was his drum-kit.

DAN takes another drink – same procedure as before.

Hawa: You haven't coughed. You sleep so much.

Rachel: Paul. I've been meaning to say, I'm thinking of moving on...

Paul: It's right here. Just up beneath your shoulder blade...

Rachel: Things haven't turned out like I thought they would.

Paul: And it's a millionth of a tone darker than the ones around it. It's a freckle that has a knack of drawing attention to itself. It's a freckle that kind of knows its power to take the eye... to delight... to tantalize. It's a bit of a tart, to be honest. A freck-whore. I love it... totally.

Silence. HAWA stops working the grain. She listens, tense and defeated.

Paul: You're leaving. I'm going to die.

Rachel: What?

Paul: You're leaving me.

Rachel: The bollocks you talk. I'm leaving the *lab*.

Paul: Oh thank God.

Rachel: Ian's so full of shit... and all I've become is a glorified technician. I've had real qualms about the embryo work – I'm really not convinced it's justified. And I'm fed up of spending my days squinting down a poxy microscope.

Paul: Thank God.

Rachel: And I'm only ever setting stuff up so that Ian can prove something that's already been done better in a hundred other places.

HAWA exits.

Paul: I thought you liked Ian.

Rachel: *You* like Ian.

Paul: That's true. He's dull and he's got a comb-over and he's no threat. I like you working with Ian.

Rachel: He's a lovely guy and everything... but he's a shit scientist. He's going to be upset about it... when he finds out.

HAWA re-enters carrying KITO, wrapped in a cloth. She cradles him gently against her shoulder.

Paul: Hey, I just thought. You could work with me, maybe... do some preparation for me, there's always things I could do with help on... research and that. It'd be brilliant.

Rachel: I'm a scientist Paul, not an artist's gofer.

Paul: Wouldn't you like to work together with me?

Rachel: Would *you* like to be my lab technician?

Paul: Would I fuck!

Rachel: Exactly. So what's the difference? Go on. Tell me.

Paul: Don't start this again.

Rachel: You think that my work's irrelevant cack, whilst you... you're on some special, life-changing journey.

Paul: I don't. (*Pause, less convinced.*) I don't. (*Pause.*) At least... I don't think what you do is shit.

Rachel: I've got a new job, anyway.

Paul: You what?

Rachel: Commercial sector, sort of.

Paul: Since when?

Rachel: GTS.

Paul: A car as well?

HAWA sings softly to KITO.

Rachel: Stop fucking about – Gene Therapy Solutions. GTS. I told you about them. They sort of... well this guy called Graham Petersen, who's a project leader for them... he kind of head-hunted me.

Paul: This is what you were thinking about... then.

Rachel: No.

Paul: Liar.

Rachel: Not really.

Dan: He used to... he used to... when he tasted something he was cooking... off a spoon... or the tip of a finger... his eyes would always shut.

Rachel (*warmer*): Tell me about my freckle. Freckle One.

Paul: It's *you* – that freckle.

PAUL kisses Freckle One.

Dan: I don't even boil an egg in this place, now. All I do is keep it clean.

HAWA holds KITO to her, absolutely still now.

Paul: You taste of salt and almost lemon... and, and vanilla in there somewhere.

Rachel: Vanilla. I love vanilla.

Paul: That'll be the freckle. A vanilla freckle.

The screen shows the successful extraction of the nucleus. DAN stands – rehearsal concluded – and moves to the tripod. He sets the camera ready to run.

Rachel: I like that.

Paul: And I *can* paint... of course I can. You don't get into the

Slade without being able to paint – and I won the prize for drawing, when I was at the RCA. Not bad for a sculptor.

Rachel: Fuck the CV. Kiss Freckle One.

Paul: Know what? I want to do life drawing again. In fact... *(he breaks away from RACHEL, looking for drawing materials within arm's length.)*

DAN sets the camera running and returns to the chair.

Rachel (*anguish*): Paul... don't stop....

Paul: I want to draw *you* – right now.

Rachel: You can draw me later. Do something three-D with me now.

PAUL returns, close to RACHEL. He holds a marker pen and an old envelope. She takes both from him.

Paul: This is not the way the muse is supposed to behave... I hope you know that.

Rachel: Shut up, you old tosser.

They kiss – long and slow.

Dan (*to the camera*): 'Taxonomy.' For Lawrence.

Hawa: Kito. I will bury you. I will bury you tonight.

Blackout.

Scene 2

Actor/Screen: Months later.

The screen shows footage from Dan's 'Taxonomy'. PAUL is watching the footage on the screen quite closely. He is on the bed. RACHEL enters the space and starts tidying around him. DAN's voice can be heard, not over-loud, running behind their dialogue until indicated.

Screen footage is an unchanging shot of DAN sitting in his chair, as we saw before. He is wrapping a copper pan in white cloth as he speaks.

Dan: Perfect, you would say, for gratin dishes. Memory serves me a summer evening, and just ourselves to enjoy it. And you had picked leaves from the kitchen garden and washed them and carefully dried each one with kitchen towel, and drizzled your thickest olive oil... oil the deep green of bottle glass... in a tiny, thumb-stopped stream. Gratin almost too hot to put in my mouth. Leaves soothing, cool and unresisting. I remember the lesion on your neck – angry. I mean it was angry-looking... makes me angry too.

Rachel: What the hell are you watching that crap for? You could do something useful.

PAUL mutes the image on the screen.

Paul: Maybe.

Rachel: Cooking programmes. Daytime shite.

Paul: It's on DVD.

Rachel: You're *buying* daytime shite on DVD! Haven't you got some work to do?

Paul: This *is* work. Someone else's. Someone called Dan... something....

Rachel: Cooking?

Paul: Well, it's not as simple as that.

HAWA re-enters the space, she carries a container of water and a flattish wooden bowl in which a dough mixture is started. The cloth is empty once more. She places the bowl and water container on the ground. She inhales the empty cloth, before spreading it out on the ground. She moves the bowl so that it is on the cloth and she sits behind it, facing out at us. Her palm kneading the dough, slowly, ruminatively.

Rachel: I didn't think it would be. And you don't know his name.

Paul: He's trying for a job. Assistant, and that. Not exactly my kind of thing, but there's something about it. I'm going to meet him. Cast an eye over him. I could do with someone to help on this new idea. Did I tell you I've had a new idea?

Rachel: There's still nothing in the fridge.

Paul: WHAT?

Rachel: Nothing edible, I mean.

Paul: So the...

Rachel: The worm casts are fine, yes.

Paul: Thank fuck.

Rachel: I thought you were going to get dinner.

Paul: And I will.

Rachel: I mean, I thought you'd have got something in by now.

Paul: I've been busy. In fact it happened today – the new idea.

Rachel: Christ, Paul, there isn't even any milk, I can't have a cup of tea.

Paul: I think we're out of tea bags, too. At least I couldn't find them.

Rachel: For FUCK'S SAKE! (*She finally has his attention.*)

Paul: Come and sit down.

Rachel: Fuck off.

Paul: No, come on. (*Silence.*) Come and snuggle up and watch this. With me. Tell me what you think.

RACHEL sits beside him – narked.

Rachel: Turn it off, will you?

PAUL freezes the image on the screen.

Paul: What's up?

Rachel: Nothing.

Paul: Had a bad day?

Rachel: No. I've had a brilliant day. I just want a cup of tea.

Paul: Oh. (*Pause.*) Graham hasn't pissed you off yet, then?

Rachel: I need to talk to you.

Paul: About Graham?

Rachel: Will you ever take a day off?

Paul: I don't really like Graham.

Rachel: You haven't even met him.

Paul: You know where you are with a comb-over.

Rachel: Graham's got a thick and lustrous mane – get over it. How long have you been watching this stuff? You smell like you've been inside all day... this bed smells like *you've* been in *it* all day, come to that.

Paul: I've been working.

Rachel: Watching someone else's work.

Paul: He's called it 'Taxonomy'. It's kind of interesting. It's kind of like a list.

Rachel (*sardonic*): What are the chances...

Paul: Eh?

Rachel: Taxonomy's one of ours. It means classification – plant types, animal types. You didn't bother to look it up.

HAWA stops working the dough. Still and silent in grief.

Paul: I knew it was something like that.

Rachel: Of course, there's no dictionary within reach of the bed, so no way could you check it out.

Paul: He's sort of made an inventory of the kitchen of a dead guy. Someone he knew well. I'm trying to work out if it's his lover, or his old man, or whatever. He talks about each piece a bit and then he wraps it carefully, like he was stowing it in a tomb, like an Egyptian or something. Everything gets to be wrapped up in the same sort of stuff – muslin, I'm guessing. And the weight and size of it becomes important... everything is important in the telling and in the careful placing. It's kind of a narrative without being exactly a story. I'm boring you.

Rachel: I'm going to Nairobi.

Paul: Oh, right. To be honest, I was beginning to bore myself, but that's a bit of an over-reaction, surely? (*Pause.*) I'll go down to Sainsbury's now and get some tea bags... and some milk.

Rachel: I'm off in a couple of weeks.

Paul: You what?

Rachel: Graham chose *me*. I'm the one who's going to Nairobi.

Paul: Nairobi?

Rachel: I'd get hell if I forgot anything to do with your stuff.

Paul: Fuck. That's only like Africa, or something.

Rachel: Kenya.

Paul: Africa. You need jabs and that.

Rachel: Yellow fever, malaria, the lot – done. Brilliant, isn't it.

Paul: And this is the miracle cure thingy... with the weird-ass genes and stuff?

Rachel: It's a waste of breath telling you anything.

Paul: I *do* remember... just not the technical stuff. Stop looking at me like that. I'm interested, okay.

Rachel: There are people turning up who seem to have some kind of immunity to HIV – people who have been constantly exposed to the virus.

Paul: Yeah-yeah-yeah. Weird-ass genes. See, I *did* remember.

Rachel: There's been a small cluster of them in Nairobi for a while... they're sex workers. Another one's turned up – in some tiny place outside the city. And I'm going out there to meet her.

Paul: What's her name?

Rachel: I... I don't know... I don't know just yet.

Paul: Find out her name... they always have these fabulous meanings – names.

Rachel: Okay. I'll ask her what her name means for you, when I meet her.

Paul: 'Cos you aren't interested in her.

Rachel: That's right. I'm just an icicle of a scientist. She might as well be a numbered specimen in a test tube, so far as I'm concerned.

Paul: Sorry.

Rachel: I'm trying to be really patient. I'm trying so hard, Paul – which, incidentally, means 'arsehole'.

Paul: I'll tell you about *my* new idea if you like. (*Pause.*) I'm going to get the tea bags.

Rachel: Why are you having such a problem with me going?

Paul: I'm not.

Rachel: In fact, with my career – full stop.

Paul: I'm not.

Rachel: Then congratulate me. Ask me what I'm going to do over there. Ask me what the project's about. Go on, take an interest.

Paul: Earl Grey... or Assam?

Rachel: Kenyan!

PAUL leaves. RACHEL stands, infuriated for a few seconds, before sitting on the bed. She is narked but still, for a moment. Then her attention wanders to the screen. She finds the remote and switches it back on, watching the silent images of DAN talking to camera.

Hawa (*softly*): I never put food in your mouth, Kito. You took milk at my breast. Nothing more. I want to make food to give you. I want your teeth to grow out of your soft, red gums and gleam white in your dark mouth. I want your white teeth to tear dough I've made for you. I want your white teeth to flash in your smile when you laugh. I want you to laugh at me, Kito, when I'm a silly old woman. I want you to tease me... break my heart with your anger and your sorrow. I want you to have children of your own with a girl who I don't like and can't ever forgive. I want to grow old and die loving you... and I want *you* to bury me without looking back. That's not much to ask, is it?

Fade to black.

Scene 3

Actor/Screen: Weeks later.

DAN leads PAUL into his kitchen – set as before, minus the kitchen gear. He stands looking around him.

Paul: I recognise this.

Dan: Like I say, I'm a bit star-struck.

Paul: The kitchen....

Dan: Paul Kennedy in my kitchen. I love what you do. You're an influence... a big influence. But that'll've been obvious. Christ, sorry, I'm blurting like a groupie.

Paul: Very bare, isn't it.

Dan (*pause*): Yes. Yeah, it is, now.

Paul: I like it.

Dan: I use it as a studio, really.

Paul: It's nice and light. No cooking.

Dan: I don't so much as boil an egg. Hopeless, I am.

Paul: It's a good piece of work.

Dan: 'Taxonomy'?

Paul: This is the chair you used.

Dan: You *liked* it?

Paul: It's why I'm here.

Dan: It *is* the chair... yes. I can't believe you liked it.

Paul (*sudden upping of energy*): Listen, Dan, I'm not going to muck you about. Here's the deal. I've a piece of work coming up and it's going to be big... pretty monumental, to tell you the truth. I'm fucking excited about it. Thing is, it's so big, I'm going to need an assistant.

Dan (*gleeful*): I'll do it.

Paul: I haven't told you what it's about yet.

Dan: I don't care. I'll do it.

Paul: Your own stuff will need to take a back seat for a while. I mean, it is big... really big. And really fucking balls-achingly exciting.

Dan: Photography?

Rich, warm state of light gradually builds around RACHEL. She is standing still. PAUL holds her laptop and a bag of equipment.

Paul: There'll be some projection. And some casting. Some work in plastics – rubber... and some secretion.

Dan: Who's doing the secreting?

Paul: I'll have to get volunteers. I can't manage the quantities I'll need by myself. I'm probably going to approach subscribers to *National Geographic*... maybe *Nature*... it's a detail.

Dan: I'm good with details.

Paul: Exactly. You can be in charge of tracking down the secretions. There's some research I'll need done, too.

Dan: You don't like research?

Paul: It's a detail thing, isn't it.

Dan: Is it site-specific?

Paul: Prepare to wet your pants.

Dan: Well?

Paul: I'm confident that, once I've got the pitch together, I'll get the Turbine Hall.

Dan (*aghast; disbelief*): Tate Modern....

Paul: It's not impossible.

Dan: How soon?

Paul: There's been a whisper for a month or so now that there's a problem with the work due in early next year. I've an inside track – it could be they need something sort of late notice. I'm pulling in a few favours, obviously.

Dan: Obviously.

Paul: You know how it is...

Dan: Turbine Hall! Massive.

Paul (*quick*): Let's put it this way, the Turbine Hall is the one place big enough... to do it justice.

Dan: And it's about mapping.

HAWA approaches, unseen by RACHEL, eyeing her suspiciously.

Paul: What?

Dan: I'm guessing.

Paul: How did you know it's about mapping?

Dan: You said *National Geographic*, I took a punt on it. That your notebook? Could I?

PAUL hands over the notebook, almost involuntarily. DAN has it open instantly – he stands pouring over it. PAUL stands watching him. DAN becomes aware of PAUL's gaze. He is instantly self-conscious.

Dan: God, sorry... I'm out of order.

Paul: No, no. You're alright.

Dan: I'm very excited.

Paul: You just went from groupie to agent in about six-point-four seconds.

Dan: I did, didn't I.

PAUL sits down.

Dan: I mean, is it alright? I want to devour this right away.

Paul: Go ahead. Just a few experiments in there. I usually start with some low-level scratching... once I've got the idea, of course.

A smile exchanged. DAN is then absorbed in PAUL's notebook. It is smallish; scribbly with tiny sketches, arrows and notes. PAUL watches him. RACHEL senses she is being watched and turns. HAWA does not move, or relax.

Rachel: I'm Rachel; Rachel Unsworth. I think you must be Hawa, is that right?

Hawa: Yes.

Rachel: Thank God. I thought I was in the wrong place. (*Pause.*) Solomon was going to tell you I might be along today. Did he not say anything?

Hawa: Solomon?

Rachel: I'm Rachel; *Dr* Unsworth. Did he perhaps call me Doctor?

Hawa: You are a doctor?

Rachel: Well yes... though not a medical practitioner. I mean, not that sort of doctor... not a medical doctor.

Hawa (*correcting*): I understand.

Rachel: Right. Sorry.

Hawa: You are the scientist.

Rachel: Yes. So Solomon did say something.

Hawa (*sceptical*): And you are a woman.

Rachel: Well, yes.

Hawa: Solomon said a doctor. Solomon said a scientist. He said nothing about a woman.

Rachel: Right.

Hawa (*a smile*): Solomon wants you.

Rachel: I'm sorry?

Hawa: That must be why he didn't say you were a woman. (*An explanation.*) He sweats when he thinks about you and so he tricks his sweat by not speaking of the one thing in his mind.

Rachel: I think you've got Solomon all wrong, Hawa...

Hawa: *Dr Unsworth*, he says. And his forehead stays dry.

Dan: The Mappa Mundi!

Paul: You know it?

Dan: Of course. There was that piece of Tan Docherty's at White Cube.

Paul: Oh... yeah... right.

Dan: Brilliant, and everything, but this is very different... different field altogether.

Paul: Yeah. Of course.

Rachel: Hawa. I want to thank you for seeing me.

Hawa: So, Solomon wants you. That's alright, no need to be scared – *I* don't want Solomon.

Rachel: I don't want him. I mean...

Hawa: He's rough with us.

Rachel: What?

Hawa: Taking our blood at his hospital. He touches us like filth. He's rough. He bruises my arm with the needle.

Rachel: Solomon is doing great work – in really difficult conditions. I'm sure he wouldn't mean any harm... he's trying to do too much on his own.

Hawa: He shouts at us like we were animals.

Rachel: I'm sure it's not easy. He's been tremendously

helpful and everything, to us... to me... to the project. Did he explain what this is all about?

HAWA offers her bare arm – wrist uppermost – to RACHEL.

Rachel: What are you doing?

Hawa: You want to take my blood for something.

Rachel: It's not like that.

Hawa: You can have whatever you find in my blood – Solomon always takes it from the vein just here. You give me the money, like Solomon promised. And then you take it away with you back to America.

Rachel: No. Not America.

HAWA rolls her sleeve down over her arm and pulls away.

Hawa: He said there would be money. He said that there were dollars. You gave the money to Solomon?

Rachel: No. I have dollars... I'm from England.

Hawa: English money's no good, is it? Solomon said there were American dollars – did he take them all?

Rachel: I have US dollars.

RACHEL unzips a pocket and produces a wad of notes. She offers them. HAWA takes them, circumspectly. She opens out one note and looks at it.

Hawa (*of the note*): Who is this?

Rachel: I don't know... some American president, I think. George Washington?

Hawa: Not one of your kings?

Rachel: Look, it says...

Hawa: *The United States of America. Fifty Dollars.* They taught us to read.

Rachel: Hawa. I'm sorry. I didn't mean anything like that...

Hawa: Our school was right down by the lake. Mother made sure I went.

Rachel: I want to help, Hawa. I'm trying to help.

Hawa: Yes. I think you are.

Rachel: You are incredibly important... you're vital... you could be absolutely... I mean, this whole research that we're doing... the treatment we hope to be able to create... I think it all depends on *you*, Hawa. If that's not enough money, tell me and I'll arrange something.

Hawa: Enough money? Enough money for what?

Silence.

Rachel: I don't know, for whatever you need. I hope...

Hawa: And what is it that you think I need, Rachel Unsworth?

Rachel: I'm sorry, I don't know.

Hawa: How could you know? Enough money to buy me out of here? So that I'll never have to go with another man?

Rachel: All I *do* know is that we're depending on you.

Hawa: My son depended on me. What am I without a child?

HAWA moves away from RACHEL who watches her a while before approaching her again.

Dan: And we're going to cast an entire human genome.

Paul: That's right... my genome.

Dan: Of course. So the viewer is walking on the Mappa Mundi...

Paul: Projected on the floor, yes.

Dan: And they're taken through this whole three-D representation of the genome.

Paul: Cast in piss, shit, blood, semen; the lot.

Dan: In some kind of tubing.

Paul: That's right. Colour coded. Sort of like the map of the underground.

Dan: Andres Serrano...

Paul: Not on this scale.

Dan: Your entire genome!

They look at one another and laugh.

Paul: Some self-portrait, eh?

Dan: How many people read *National Geographic*?

PAUL shrugs. DAN looks further through the notebook.

Rachel: Solomon told me about your little boy.

Hawa (*harsh, low*): Said how I buried him and then went back to work, right away. Kito, warmer in the ground than *I* was beneath the next man... and the next.

Rachel (*low*): I'm so sorry, Hawa. (*Pause.*) Look, this isn't the time, I can see that. I'll go now. But I could be back tomorrow, if you change your mind... or the day after that. My flight's not 'til then. I want to explain to you, if you'll give me the chance. I want to tell you what we're trying to do. And how you can help us... if you're willing... how you can help us to stop women, men... and children, from dying.

Hawa: Save your breath.

Rachel: I think it's a real shame you see it that way.

Hawa: I know what you want from me. I'm *not* infected, and

I *should* be – of all people, I should be dead. Solomon told me, when he took my blood and did his spells on it over and over again. I have the bullet.

Rachel: The bullet?

Hawa: The *magic bullet* he called it. And you are going to take my blood... and find the bullet and shoot everyone with it... because that might save them.

Rachel: Is that what Solomon said?

Hawa: He wouldn't say it like a story to *you*... he's trying to impress you.

Rachel (*smiling*): I'll try to remember that, thanks.

Hawa: I don't believe Solomon's stories.

Rachel: But there *is* something amazing going on in your body, Hawa. There's got to be a reason why you're still clear. There's got to be something giving you immunity.

Hawa: I'm not immune. I've got it. I know.

Rachel: The tests show otherwise. You're HIV negative – you're antibody negative. (*Pause.*) Sorry, I'm being all hopelessly technical – no help. Look, it's just that the tests show something's really out of the ordinary.

Hawa: It's just fear.

Rachel: I don't get it.

Hawa: My fear is so strong – stronger than HIV. (*Pause.*) My fear has been protecting me. But it couldn't save Kito. My fear must be all for myself – what kind of a woman can I be?

Rachel: I don't understand...

Hawa: Maybe you haven't ever been frightened. Frightened that you will be infected. Frightened that everyone will reject you. Frightened that people will refuse to touch you... refuse to touch your baby when he falls sick and he needs their help. My fear kept the tests negative – that's all.

Rachel: Fear's a feeling. The magic bullet is something you could touch – a chemical.

Hawa (*smiling*): If you don't want Solomon, just tell him about your baby.

Rachel: My baby? I haven't got a baby.

HAWA turns to her and stands close to her, gazing into her eyes.

Hawa: A doctor... who doesn't know when she's pregnant.

Rachel (*tighter*): I'm not pregnant.

Hawa: Oh, you *are*, Rachel Unsworth, you are.

RACHEL breaks her gaze and busies herself with her bag.

Rachel: You're willing to give a blood sample now?

Hawa: I'm taking your money, Doctor Rachel. So, yes.

RACHEL extracts sterilized equipment. Syringes and containers for them. She puts on gloves and goggles. HAWA presents her arm, as before. RACHEL performs this act very carefully – focused and dispassionate. HAWA stares at her throughout the procedure.

Dan: This cube.

Paul: I want it suspended in the air... in the Turbine Hall.

Dan: And how will the viewer get inside it?

Paul: Purpose-built tubular walkways... ideally from the third level.

Dan: But the cube is also transparent.

Paul: So people anywhere with a vista on the Turbine Hall will be able to see into it. I hope that with the movement of viewers inside, the whole thing will sort of throb.

Dan: Be alive.

Paul: Crazy, isn't it. But I know it's right. It just feels absolutely right and now.

Dan: Beautiful. It's beautiful. When do I start?

They smile at one another and then leave the space.

Rachel: Did I hurt you?

Hawa: No.

Rachel: Good.

Hawa: What will you name your baby?

Rachel: I keep telling you, I'm not pregnant.

Hawa: You have a man back in America?

Rachel: London. Yes.

RACHEL stows the sample in the bag.

Hawa: Will he be a good father?

Rachel: Paul! A father? He'd be terrible.

Hawa: He has nothing... no land?

Rachel: He's an artist.

HAWA laughs, delightedly.

Hawa: He makes pictures of you.

Rachel: Not exactly.

Hawa: So he's not even a good enough artist to do that.

Rachel: He's a great artist. Very successful and quite famous... in London.

Hawa: I would like to see London. Unless it's like Nairobi...

Rachel: It's kind of different.

Hawa: If I went to London, he would make a picture of me, I think.

Rachel: Maybe, yes.

Hawa: He will love the child, Rachel.

Rachel: Would he?

HAWA opens the money into a fan.

Hawa: I couldn't buy a house in London with this, could I?

Rachel: No. That wouldn't be enough.

Hawa: How much did your house cost?

Rachel: I don't have a house. I mean, I don't own one.

Hawa: I will build my mother a new house, at home... by the lake.

HAWA grabs RACHEL and hugs her almost fiercely.

Hawa: Find the magic bullet, Doctor Rachel.

Rachel: I'll try.

Slow fade to black.

Scene 4

Actor/Screen: Days later.

Lights reveal, in her laboratory, RACHEL sitting, vacant. Palely lit. She holds a slip of paper in her hand. Daylight floods Paul's studio – PAUL and DAN, surrounded by their work. PAUL holds a slip of paper in his hand.

Paul (*cold fury*): Wankers.

Dan: We could get an architect in, no problem. It could be very exciting to get someone else on board.

Paul: Short-sighted tossers.

Dan: Or a structural engineer. It's easy enough. I'll make a few calls.

Paul (*low*): Dan. You don't get it. They could have said anything, they just chose the 'it's-not-practicable' line because it's the softest option. They have to offer a reason – it's only polite. So, (*reading*) 'Major implications for the structure and fabric of the building' was the way to go. They said no and that's it. The fact is they don't want to engage with what the piece is about. They don't understand what the piece is saying about life... about art... about science. It's too much bother to find out. (*He balls the paper and throws it aside.*)

Dan: But this is going to be brilliant. Absolutely fantastic. I can see it in my head. All of it.

PAUL rummages in a bag.

Paul: That's because *you* have imagination. *They* have spreadsheets instead...

Dan: What are you doing?

A mobile emerges from Paul's bag.

Paul: Their hearts have been replaced by the latest Pentium Processor so that they can say 'No', in a shorter time. Phoning Rachel.

Dan: Oh, right.

Paul: She'll want to know.

Rachel's mobile rings. She picks up the phone, looks at the screen and then just lets it ring.

Dan: You want to tell her.

Paul: She'll want to know.

Dan: We shouldn't let this project go. The Turbine Hall isn't the only big space in the world.

Paul: Answer then. Fuck it!

Dan: Hereford Cathedral.

Paul (*low*): Great.

Dan: Paul, don't you see? Hereford Cathedral – it would be ideal. Better than the Tate.

Paul: What are you talking about?

Dan: The Mappa Mundi connection. That's where it is – the original. So why not. Must be a huge space to work in. And the church will buy it big time. The map of man in the house of his creator.

Paul: Dan. There's one big problem with Hereford Cathedral. It's not in London.

Dan: Saint Paul's then.

Paul: And there's another thing: I don't believe in that 'creator' thing.

Dan: Curator, then.

RACHEL focuses on the paper in her hand. She reads it closely. She picks up her mobile and dials. PAUL puts his mobile back in the bag.

Dan: You could leave her a message.

Paul: I don't do messages. She'd know something was wrong if I left her a message. It'd worry her.

Rachel (*low*): Hi. It's Rachel Unsworth. I phoned earlier. That's right... it's about the termination. I've decided. I need to go ahead... the sooner the better, yes.

Black out.

Scene 5

Actor/Screen: Days later.

HAWA – night-lit.

Hawa: Rachel Unsworth. I want to tell you about your dollars – *my* dollars. *My* magic bullets. I fire them whenever I want. I am back home. With my mother. She wants a new house and already I'm firing magic bullets to build her one. We can see the lake from where we are. We buy fish from the fishermen... with *money*. I was only a girl when I bought my first fish – without money. My father was sick, my brother was sick and we had to eat, Rachel Unsworth. The fisherman made me cry, even though he wasn't rough with me – I know that now. He stank. His breathing got wild above me. And he had a fever. The blue sky swung above my head – the boat kept straining on the rope he'd tied off at the shore. Mother never asked me how I got the fish. (*Pause.*) We sing when we are cooking together. I keep thinking that it's a memory I'm having of being a child. But it's *real*. Good times. Just mother and me. In the night, when she is tired, I stroke her head and sing her lullabies until she sleeps. Then I come outside and look at the sky. And always then... always then I can feel the gap inside my body – right here, up under my heart... a gap the exact size and shape of Kito. A gap that weighs one hundred times his weight. (*Pause.*) I drink Coca-Cola. Whenever I want. Such sweetness. (*Pause.*) I'm thinking about you and your baby, right now, Rachel Unsworth. Don't let him be named 'Guedado' – *unwanted*. You could call him 'Kito' – it means *precious*.

The flat. RACHEL flicks a lighter and sets a tea-light going. For a moment it seems as if she and HAWA are in eye contact. A gradual building of light in this area of the space shows that RACHEL, PAUL and DAN are sitting among the remains of an ad hoc meal. HAWA stays in the space. A calm presence. She lies on her back looking up at the night sky. She hums softly to herself. She produces a can of Coca-Cola.

Dan: That was brilliant.

Rachel: Yeah, right.

Dan: I *mean* it.

Rachel: I thought you were into *proper* food. All those copper pans of yours.

Paul: School-girl error, Rachel, confusing the artist with the art.

Dan: No, I love junk food. It was Lawrence that was. Thanks anyway.

Rachel: I went to a lot of trouble.

Paul: Went as far as the carry-out Greek on the corner.

PAUL throws DAN another can of beer.

Dan: Cheers. (*To Rachel:*) Will you get to go back to Nairobi?

Rachel: I hope so.

Paul (*playful*): You've hardly been here a week... and most of that she's spent in the lab.

Rachel: There's a lot to do.

Paul: She's gone for days on end.

Rachel: One over-nighter. That's all. Time to myself in there is vital. No distractions. *You* disappear often enough.

Paul: That's different.

Rachel (*playful*): A fortnight in a wigwam in Coventry. Different's not the word.

Dan: 'I-Reservation'?

Paul: That's right. Did you see it?

Dan: Of course. I brought Lawrence. He loved it. (*To Rachel:*) It was an installation.

HAWA fizzes open the can of Coca-Cola. She sips from it. The taste makes her smile.

Paul: Don't fall for it, Dan. She understands perfectly well what it was and why I was there.

Rachel (*firm*): But *you* neither know, understand nor care what my work is about.

Paul: Bollocks.

Rachel (*high-horsing*): 'I-Reservation' – an installation consisting of a self-made bivouac created out of two weeks' household waste produced by the Sinclair family of Yarnley Drive, Coventry, occupied by the artist, as an exploration of late twentieth-century consumerism. Now tell Dan what my research is about.

Paul: Alright. I will.

Rachel: This ought to be worth listening to... if you've got your camera, Dan, start it rolling now.

Paul: A dodgy bunch of scientists, funded by an even dodgier US pharmaceutical multinational, is trying to exploit the AIDS epidemic.

Rachel (*darker*): You are such a twat.

Paul: So they send Rachel to collect some sort of DNA, that she's come home to tamper with, raiding dozens of embryos for stem cells.

Rachel: You *know* that's untrue.

Paul: So that she can help formulate some sort of drug, which may or may not have a success rate as high as thirty per cent. The drug will then be marketed at a price too high for the people it might actually help.

Dan (*low*): I didn't know it was to do with HIV.

Rachel: That's about the only thing arse-face got right.

Dan: So what is it, then?

Rachel (*pause*): We're mainly government-funded. Christ almighty, why am I starting with that.

Dan: Maybe it matters where the money comes from.

Rachel: The only thing that matters is finding out whatever we can.

Dan (*low, sceptical*): Discovering a cure? Like that's gonna happen.

Rachel: 'Cure' is too emotive a word.

Dan: So what's the point?

Rachel: There are people who seem to be HIV immune. I mean, long-term exposed but uninfected.

Dan (*cold*): I know.

Rachel: There's a cluster of them around Nairobi. I went to take samples of DNA from the latest donor to be found.

Paul: And you still don't know any of their names.

Rachel: Hawa. In Kiswahili it means *longing*. She works in truck stops outside Nairobi. She's been a prostitute for eight years. So she's been continuously exposed to HIV – but she's still negative. She thinks she's got the virus, but the tests are unequivocal. She's not a long-term non-progressor, she's the real thing – she's immune. She's completely in the clear.

Dan: What makes her think she's got it?

Rachel (*tightening all the time now*): Her baby son died, and she's convinced herself it was of AIDS... and that she transmitted it to him through her breast milk... but she can't have done.

Dan: Didn't they test the baby?

Rachel: Solomon told me she wouldn't let anyone touch him – buried him herself.

Dan: So no one knows.

Rachel: Something else killed him... it was just a little while ago. It could have been anything. He only lived a few months, and all that time in poverty. He was at risk from anything.

Paul: Maybe.

Rachel (*low*): I know his name, too, Paul... and I know what it means... but if you make me say any of that... Jesus Christ, now she's going to start crying.

Paul (*warm*): Hey... sweetheart... what is it?

Rachel: And just for the record...

Paul (*warmer*): What happened over there?

Rachel (*choked*): Just for the record, Paul, there's no embryo work involved in anything I do, now. Okay?

Paul: Okay. Sorry.

DAN is looking away.

Rachel (*calming*): What I'm doing, Dan. What I'm doing... is analysing her DNA, sequencing it... looking for a mutation... a mutation that might be making her immune. Somewhere in there, something's making her body create the proteins right now that are protecting her. It's important.

Hawa: Coca-Cola... sweet enough to hurt. Sweet enough to hurt.

Paul (*an apology*): I'm thinking of cutting my genitals off... sort of a twenty-first century riposte to Van Gogh. What do you think?

Blackout.

Scene 6

Actor/Screen: Hours later.

Rachel's lab. RACHEL stands facing DAN. He holds a bunch of flowers.

Rachel (*tight*): There was no need for those. And I've nothing to put them in, except the sink.

Dan: Oh, right. Didn't think. (*Pause.*) Got a few funny looks I did, coming in here.

Rachel: I'm not surprised.

Dan: That tall Aussie, in the other room...

Rachel: Graham? He's a New Zealander.

Dan: Thought I was Paul, I think. Some scowl he's got on him.

Rachel: He can be a bit territorial.

Dan: About you?

Rachel: About the *lab*. Anyway, he's met Paul.

Dan: That must have been interesting.

Rachel: Nobody punched anybody. But it wasn't for want of trying.

Dan: Can't picture Paul actually coming to blows.

Rachel: I meant *I* didn't punch either of them.

Dan: Right. So, this is where it all goes on.

Rachel: You don't have to pretend to be interested.

Dan (*warmer*): I'm not pretending. (*Pause.*) Look. Rachel, I didn't want to get off on the wrong foot with you. And I'm here to tell you that I'm sorry about what I said.

Rachel: You didn't say anything... except 'no'.

Dan: I didn't explain very well.

Rachel: You're perfectly entitled to say no. It's your DNA. Hawa could have done the same – it's no different.

Dan: But I want to explain about refusing to help... about not letting you take a blood sample from me.

Rachel: It's fine. Forget it.

Dan: I guess I was a bit fazed to find out that your research is kind of about me. Paul and me... well, I've always kept the talk about our work... and he never exactly said what your field was.

Rachel: Here's my surprised face.

Dan: He talks about you all the time, if you're interested. (*Pause.*) Well, a lot of the time. He's not all that work-obsessed really.

Rachel: We're both passionate about what we do. There's nothing wrong in that – Paul doesn't need defending on that score.

Dan: Right. Not for me to defend him either.

Rachel: Exactly. I think he's enjoyed having you around.

Dan: It's been great for me. But it's over with now. White Cube rejected the pitch... did he tell you?

Rachel: Would they be the 'Smug fuckwits' he was referring to this morning?

Dan: Probably. And it really isn't worth scaling it down any further.

Rachel: Maybe you can collaborate on something else.

Dan: Do you really think he'd consider it?

Rachel: Oh, I don't know, he doesn't discuss that kind of thing with me... but you seem to be good together, don't you.

Dan: God, I'd love to work with him again. (*Pause.*) Some kit you've got in here.

Rachel: It's where I do my cooking.

Dan: That's an odd word for it.

Rachel: I think a lot of the time it's exactly the *right* word. Managing ingredients... sort of adjusting to taste, judging the moment when it's ready.... A lot of similarities.

Dan: And what was that weird thing Russell Crowe was pouring over, next door – sort of like a cappuccino machine, only huge?

Rachel: That'd be the electron microscope.

Dan: Go on then, blind me.

Rachel: It bombards the stuff. You have to prepare the specimens so that they reflect electrons, or else you won't get a thing. They have to be coated in gold... and then a magnet focuses the electrons onto whatever it is and you're away.

Dan: So there's no mirrors and stuff?

Rachel: No point. There's no light.

Dan: But you can still see. How weird is that? (*Awkward.*) Look...

Rachel: It's okay, Dan. I'm fine about it. There's nothing you have to justify.

Dan: It's just... Lawrence was so ill for so long... and I spent all that time with him. He was ill all through our relationship.

Rachel: That's something I *do* want to ask you.

Dan: Sorry?

Rachel: I don't get why you put yourself at risk like that with him.

Dan (*aggressive; arch*): Why didn't I *use protection*?

Rachel: Well, yes. That was crazy.

Dan: Been bare-backing on and off before I met him. I was in San Francisco for a couple of years... it was a thing I did there. Lots of people did.

Rachel: Insane.

Dan: Judgemental.

Rachel: Fair enough. (*Pause.*) Sorry, okay?

Dan: Forget about it.

Rachel: Dan, I *do* want to know.

Dan: *Do* you?

Rachel: Please.

Dan: Whether it was right or wrong, that's what I did. It's kind of a marker; putting down a marker. Saying, 'Fuck it, this is me'. Not compromising. I'm justifying myself, now.

Rachel: That's my fault.

Dan: It is, you cow. (*Pause.*) Look, Rachel, by the time I met him, I kind of already thought of myself as being damned or immortal, depending on my mood. But Lawrence was always upfront about it... about being HIV positive. I didn't want anything in the way. So I told him I was too. I think I kind of wanted it to be true, and for all I knew then it *was* true.... That's fucked up, I know.

Rachel: Crazy bastard.

Dan: Risk *is* sexy, isn't it? And when you love someone like that. Like I loved that cantankerous old prick.... I didn't care what happened to me. (*Pause.*) Rachel, I wanted to be so close to him – superimposed on him. Well, you know.

Rachel: Maybe.

Dan: You're fooling no one.

Rachel: So you've had tests.

Dan: Not until after he died. But regularly since. Still negative. I've had people going on at me about this gene thing before. There's some study into immunity running out of UCL, is it? Our GP really pressured me to get involved... but, well... I didn't.

Rachel: Right. (*Edgy.*) I got really emotional and out of order last night. And said things I shouldn't.... No, fuck it. I said what was right. I just didn't do it very well. Dan, you could be part of a real advance in treatment. This isn't some cloud-cuckoo thing we're doing here. The more DNA we can access from people who show immunity, the better our chances get.

Dan: I have it in my power to add to the sum total of human happiness.

Rachel: Well, yes. You do. So why not?

Dan: It's just... I dunno. I just don't feel like doing it. Some people carry donor cards for everything, others faint at the thought of having a dead eye taken out of their dead skull.

Rachel (*cold*): It's not going to hurt giving up a DNA sample.

Dan: I know. I somehow don't want to find out... don't want it to be known why I'm clear. I don't want it written down in numbers and graphs and stuff. I want my mystery intact. Is that monumentally selfish of me or something?

Rachel: It's nothing to do with being selfish, Dan. I just don't think you like yourself that much.

Dan: Fuck off.

Rachel: No, I mean it. I think you've got a problem.

Dan: Fucking psychobabble.

Rachel: I thought to start with that you were still just grieving.

Dan: I'm going, now.

Rachel: I thought Hawa was going to refuse me for just that reason. She's only buried her baby and we're all over her. Pestering her for her blood. Waving money in her face like that made it okay. I've never felt so humiliated, giving her cash for that.

DAN focused hopelessly on the flowers in his hands.

Dan: *He* liked me. That was enough. I'm going now. Do you want these fucking things or not?

Rachel: Thanks. (*She takes them.*)

Dan: You can dip them in gold and plunge them in the dark and explode their mystery when I'm gone.

Rachel: There's no need. We know everything there is to know about freesias already. Unlike HIV. Alright, so you've finally worked out that Lawrence loved you – would he like you if he knew what you were refusing to do now? Would he?

Dan: This is none of your business.

Rachel: And then you find out that all the time you were carrying something in your DNA that could have saved him.

Dan: Christ!

Rachel: So because it's too late for Lawrence, everyone else can go fuck themselves.

Dan: Rachel, shut up.

Rachel: If Lawrence was still alive, no way would you be refusing.

Dan (*blurting*): He'd only be awake for an hour or so, at the end. Is this want you want to hear? We did these pictures together. Sort of. I'd take his finger and dip it in ink and paint with his finger... stupid little things... daubs. And when he was asleep I'd work at them with a fine-liner... sort of turn them into cartoons... about him and me. Stories, kind of. And the next time he woke up I'd show him what we'd made between us. And he'd say they were *moronic*, or something. I was doing that when he died – daubing with his dead finger for a while, before I realised that he'd gone. Is that what you have to know? Grieving. Of course I'm grieving. I'm not ready. I'm not ready for the world and its huge stuff. All the big things look small from this side of the lens. That's it.

Silence.

Dan: It's such a bastard disease. Such a bastard.

Rachel (*brighter*): Wanna see something? Wanna see *my* pictures? (*She punches up some work on her lap top.*)

Rachel: This is Hawa's DNA.

Dan (*glances briefly*): Colourful.

Rachel (*clicks again*): And this is the area that *we're* interested in.

Dan: How did you make this?

Rachel (*points at the laptop screen*): There's an anomaly here. In this part of the sequence. I say it's a mutation, Graham says it's inconclusive. But if I'm right, if this is something to do with why she's still clear, then we might have found an opening.

Dan: So you think you might be there already?

Rachel: No way. There's tons more detail to go into. (*Pause.*) And we need further samples, of course. What would be brilliant would be finding another donor with a similar mutation. And, of course then we'd be done. We'd pass our findings on... so the parent company can develop a treatment. Field tests. And then, maybe...

Dan (*of the screen*): It's beautiful. How's it done?

Rachel: This? It's just a sequencing graph. Stuff with gels and dyes. It's what DNA sequencers cough up.

Dan: So this is what you were up to on your over-nighter.

Rachel (*tight*): Time on the sequencer's like gold dust. (*Smiles.*) I've hard copies somewhere, if you want to take one with you.

DAN remains looking at the laptop screen.

Rachel (*pause*): Dan. Promise me you'll have another think about taking part.

Dan: Maybe.

Rachel (*light*): I've a good mind to call Graham in here right now and grass you up to him.

Dan: Will he grab me and hold me down while you do the business with the syringes or whatever?

Rachel: He might if you asked nicely.

Dan: I'll see you.

Rachel: Thanks for dropping by. And thanks for the flowers.

Fade to black.

Scene 7

Actor/Screen: Days later.

HAWA in warm, evening light. She has a bowl of water and collard greens. PAUL in the flat. He has his mobile. He dials a number. A phone starts ringing. It takes him a moment to realise it's in the flat.

Hawa: I want your life, Rachel Unsworth. I want a Paul. An artist.

Paul: Oh, great, Rachel, that's a new one. (*He starts hunting the ringing mobile. Looking through detritus. Getting nowhere. The phone stops as her voicemail cuts in.*)

Hawa: He'd see me on the train like he first saw you.

Paul: For Christ's sake. (*He dials again. Waits, infuriated by the ring tone, and starts hunting once more. This time he tracks it down to her bag. He takes it out as it stops ringing and holds both phones.*)

Hawa: And I'd be nose in a book, not seeing him. Just like you were. (*She takes a handful of collard leaves and dunks it into the water. She lifts it out, shakes the water off, and keeps her hand suspended over the bowl so that the leaves can continue to drip.*)

Paul (*chiming in*): 'Hi... you've reached Rachel but I'm not able to take your call right now,' that would be because you've gone to work without the fucking thing you daft... (*leaving a message:*) yeah, Rachel, I wanted to talk to you because I'm feeling a bit pissed off and because you are my significant other you might have been some help. (*Pause.*) 'Significant other...' – I hate simpering shite like that. Look, Rachel I love you and I need you. And I want to hear your voice right now... not your poxy recorded message. And now I come to think of it, I'm kind of paranoid that you didn't take your phone *deliberately* so I couldn't reach you and that you are having hot angry Antipodean sex with Graham or whatever he's called right now. (*He ends the call. He sits with both phones in his hands. He is looking at Rachel's phone. After a moment he starts pressing the keys. To listen to his own message.*)

Paul: Fuck. Best listen to that again. Don't want to come over hysterical or something.... (*He listens, with a grim satisfaction, to his own message.*)

Hawa: And he'd just stare so hard at me, and then he'd start singing the words I was reading... so I'd have to notice him. And I'd look up. And smile at this crazy man singing the words of my book that weren't written for singing. And I'd say yes. He can make a picture of me. Whenever he wants.

Once it is over, PAUL sits for a moment, still looking at Rachel's phone.

Paul: Who else leaves you messages like that, Rachel... who else leaves you messages? (*He starts to listen to other messages on her voicemail.*)

Hawa: I think we would have many babies, my Paul and me. Strong babies who run and laugh and shout.

A message makes PAUL start. He stands, agitated and listens to it again.

Paul (*low*): Jesus. (*He picks up the bag and empties the contents onto the floor. He scrabbles through the stuff there, reading scraps of paper, correspondence. One official-looking letter takes his attention. He slips the paper out of the envelope. Stilled. Cold. He reads it.*) You've got to be kidding. (*He storms across the space.*)

Blackout.

Scene 8

Actor/Screen: An hour later.

PAUL's storming brings him into the space with RACHEL. Light reveals DAN in his kitchen. He holds the finger painting book in his hands. He is turning over the pages, slowly, smiling.

Paul (*raging*): I can't believe you'd just treat your own body like it's a fucking Agar plate...

Rachel: Oh, behave.

Paul: And you cut me out. Literally. Cut me out of it. Cut me out of you. You go creeping off to some poxy private clinic. You don't tell me... you don't ever tell me anything about it. I have rights.

Rachel: So do I.

Paul: Don't give me that 'it's my body' shite.

Rachel: It *is* my body.

Paul: Not *all* of it. I can just see how it was. You find out you're pregnant and it's 'oh no, that's not part of the plan... but, hey, no worries, it can be dealt with.'

Rachel: That's bollocks.

Paul: Hey, it can be disappeared. Nothing to it... a bit of physics, or a bit of chemistry, will take care of all that messy biology. You spend half your working life dicking about with embryos, and our child was just another bunch of expendable stem cells....

DAN produces a mobile and punches numbers.

Rachel: Paul...

Paul: Plenty more where they came from...

Rachel: That's not how it was.

Rachel's mobile ring tone is heard. She goes towards her bag but PAUL grabs her.

Paul: Don't even think about taking that call. I just can't believe you went ahead like that without talking to me. You never gave me a thought, did you? Did you!

Rachel: When have you ever mentioned children?

Paul: That's not the point.

Rachel: You haven't the slightest idea what went through my head.

Paul: Like you'd tell me.

Rachel: I'm telling you *now*.

Paul: Nothing about me, that's for sure.

Rachel: Oh, I thought about you alright. There was one thing I was certain about. And that was that if I wanted to keep it you'd run away screaming. You'd have said 'terminate'.

Dan: Bloody voicemail!

Paul: The fucking arrogance!

Rachel: You'd have said terminate just like that, because there's no room in your life for a baby. You don't want a baby.

Paul: Bollocks.

Rachel: You've never talked about wanting children.

Paul: I want one now. The one you've got rid of.

Rachel: Paul...

Paul: I want our one. Christ. It's alright for you, you've got your eggs all safely stowed away, a little private arsenal of pearls.

Dan: Hi, Rachel. It's Dan. I changed my mind. Give us a call. (*He rings off and stows the phone away, picks up a rolled A3 sheet, unfurls it and looks at it. It is the sequencing picture. He sits and looks at it, deep in thought. Then he starts making notes.*)

Paul (*lower*): I'm not sure that my sperm are even any good at this age.

Rachel: You're only thirty-six, you twat. Loads of men father kids into their forties and fifties.

Paul: Sperm degenerate. Mine could all be freaks with two

heads and no tails by now. You don't know.

Rachel: Well one of them was gymnastic enough a few weeks ago.

Paul: Hang on, hang on. How do I even know that it was mine?

Rachel: This conversation is over.

Paul: It fucking isn't. You're screwing Graham aren't you? I knew it.

Rachel: Jesus!

Paul: You've been different since that job came up. You've been different since you started working there... with him. And when you came back from Nairobi, you totally changed.

Rachel: I'd just been to the Third World – it changes everyone. It fucking well should. God. What's the point....
(*She picks up her bag and makes for the door.*)

Paul: Where are you going?

Rachel: Back to work.

Paul: You're not.

Rachel: That's right, I forgot. I'm not going to work. I'm going to shag Graham in a ritual circle of lit Bunsen burners while we chant the periodic table.

Paul: Cow.

Silence.

Rachel (*calmer*): Look, Paul, I've time booked on the sequencer...

Paul: Fuck the sequencer. We're talking.

Rachel: You're shouting. That's all that's happening here. And you aren't listening. So I'm going somewhere calm and quiet and useful. You can shout to yourself. Get it out of your system.

Paul: We are in serious trouble.

Rachel: I'll see you later.

Paul: Yeah right.

Rachel: And then you can apologise for going through my stuff. Not to mention presuming to know what I think and what I feel.

Paul: I don't presume to know any such thing. That's exactly the point. That's the thing I *want* to know. I want to know what you feel. And I want that baby.

Rachel: You want to control me. That's all. Be honest, can't you? *I* took a decision for once and you hated *that*. It could have been about anything.

Paul: I want a child – with you.

Rachel: You're exactly the same with my work.

Paul: Christ! You and your fucking work.

Rachel: It's important. It's part of me.

Paul: Our baby was part of you.

Silence.

Rachel (*low*): Prick.

Paul: Nothing must terminate your precious work, Rachel, must it?

Rachel: You think you're in a relationship with that girl you saw on the underground, years ago... and who you kidded yourself you were in love with – just like that! So fucking poetic – just like that. As if.

Paul: That's how pheromones work, you're always telling me – you can't shut them out... they take you unawares... they take over.

Rachel: You had a completed idea of me on that train.

Paul (*lower*): You talk utter shite.

Rachel: There's more to me than that girl on the train. More to me... *and less*. That's the truth of it. Just like there's a lot more to you than an artist who's right up himself.

Paul (*lower*): Thanks.

Rachel: Oh, Paul... how can you think I'm not sorry about the termination? I feel sorry and guilty and ashamed.

Paul (*listless*): I'm useless.

Rachel: You're not. Not useless. Infantile, self-obsessed maybe... but not useless.

Paul: Make use of me, then... now. I want to make usefulness to you now.

DAN stops his frantic sketching and looks up – an epiphany.

Dan (*softly*): Paul. (*He looks around as if expecting PAUL to be there, re-collects himself and fishes out the mobile again. He waits a moment – a decision.*)

Rachel: Paul.

Paul: Go on. I've got an evolutionary imperative on right now.

Rachel: You've been angry so you've got excited. That's all. I'm going to work. Why don't you do the same?

Paul: Don't tell me when I'm going to work.

Rachel (*picks up her bag, removes the mobile and scrutinizes it for the missed call*): You wanted me as your assistant once. Remember?

Paul: I still do.

Rachel: Only so you could control me; not so that I could be part of the precious creative process. (*Triumph – of the mobile.*) Wow.

Paul: Who was it that called? Graham, I suppose.

Rachel: Dan. (*She listens to the message.*)

Paul: What the fuck does Dan have to say to you?

Silence.

Rachel (*beaming*): He's going to take part.

Paul (*bitter*): So he's *your* assistant now. Congratulations.

Rachel: Don't be idiotic. And get on with your work.

Paul: For the last time, stop telling me how to do my work.

Rachel: Oh, right. You can pronounce on mine, but I mustn't presume...

Paul: Fucking shut up!

Rachel: And, come to think of it, why's your stuff suddenly using science?

Paul: The Mappa Mundi project was a good idea.

Rachel: You don't give a toss about the Human Genome. It was just a new colour in your paint box...

Paul: Those Tate Modern arseholes!

Rachel: They didn't commission you because it wasn't good enough.

Paul: Fuck off!

Rachel: And it wasn't good enough because you aren't passionate about it. If you were you wouldn't have had Dan doing pathetic, half-arsed Google searches for you. If you'd wanted to know anything about it you could have asked me – I'm an expert, remember? It's not a million miles away from my field.

Paul: You haven't a clue what you're talking about. You don't know how I develop stuff.

Rachel: Why don't you make a piece of work about what you're *really* passionate about?

Paul: You're making a dick of yourself now.

Rachel: Develop some stuff about controlling me.

Paul: Go to work, Rachel.

Rachel: Do something that's about you choking the life out of me.

RACHEL leaves the space. PAUL screams a single shout of rage, then he folds down, in on himself. Paul's mobile starts ringing. After a couple of seconds he darts for it.

Dan: Can you talk!

Paul: What the fuck are you playing at, Dan?

Dan: Is Rachel there?

Paul: I said...

Dan: I've had an idea. Is Rachel there? Can you talk?

Blackout.

Scene 9

Actor/Screen: Weeks later.

HAWA is sorting and packing French beans. It is mind-bendingly tedious. She is deft – automatic and blank of expression. RACHEL is in the lab. She has pages of sequencer graphs: one set from Hawa's DNA, the other from Dan's. The image of PAUL and DAN – the latter is filming – is picked up on the screen above.

Paul: We met on the tube; in a tube – an irony that escaped me at the time. She was doing that tube thing... you know... folded into herself, reading – some scientific paper. Rush hour. We're all crammed up against one another. So you don't even need to hang on to a handle, or anything, you can just gently lean and bounce off this collective human cushion. And everyone is being totally English about it. Desperately trying to avoid, or deny the physical contact. And hilariously silent. Got the giggles, didn't I. And she was... right here, her side jutting into me. My eyes are about three inches from her temple. And I don't bother to not stare. (*Pause.*) She's beautiful. And she's ignoring me even though, when the train lurches to the left, I can feel her right breast buffering the ribs beneath my heart.

RACHEL spots a correlation. She can't quite believe it. A frantic leafing through – she extracts two sheets. Looks again.

Paul: I can't bear it. I say something. I dunno, something like, 'Stinking, aren't I.' And she does the deaf thing. So I get ambitious....

Rachel: What... (*She looks up – a flush of excitement. She is breathing deep. Slowly, she resumes her scrutiny of the sheets.*)

Paul: 'That looks dead interesting...' and still she ignores me. So I start singing it, the words on her page. Kind of make a cakey ballad out of these tables of data. She blushes. So I go straight into a second verse. Other people are edging away, an inch or two around us, here and there. And I just carry on singing. And eventually she lowers the paper, turns to me and looks at me. And I ask her if I can take a photo of her left eye, which has tiny flecks of gold among the darkness there. Eventually, she realises she's got to answer. Her first word to me: 'Why?' What a scientist, eh? 'Why?' So I explain that she just gave me an idea for a piece about viewing. It became 'Eye-I', eventually.

Rachel: Almost identical. (*Softly:*) Graham.

Paul: Sort of turned a small space at Danielle Miro into a microscope. Thing is... the thing is... I'm crap at everything, not just singing. Evolution says I'm crap – expendable – because I'm a man. She told me once that the point of the male, in evolutionary terms – which are the only ones which have any weight for her – that the point of the male had been to fertilize the ovum, and that *now* science has found ways of doing that without us. She said...

Rachel (*louder*): Graham! Come here!

Paul: She said inception – that first impulse, the one which turns an egg into an embryo – can be achieved by introducing a small electrical charge. That's all we ever were, men, just a couple of volts, or something. Not even enough to turn over the starter motor of a family saloon, oh, no. Just about enough juice to change channels.

Rachel (*laughing and shouting*): GRAHAM! (*To self:*) Fucking amazing. Unbelievable!

Paul: That's it. So of course she aborted our baby. A bit of DNA from anyone she takes a fancy to, and she can zap herself one another day... when it suits her... when she's finished her beautiful work... when she's moved the sum of human knowledge up a notch or two... and, as a kind of collateral relief-stroke-damage, tweaked the current stats on the sum of human happiness one way or another.

PAUL sits, impassive. DAN looks at him for a moment and then switches the camera off.

Dan: Yeah, good. That looked great.

Screen blanks.

Paul: I want to try it again.

Dan: Let's look at it first.

Paul: But I want to do it again.

Dan: There's lots of time. Watch first.

Paul: Go on then.

Dan: Here...

DAN turns the camera around. PAUL and DAN crowd the viewing screen. They share a pair of ear-phones.

Paul: That bit.

Dan: What? The 'her first word' thing?

Paul: Looks too weak. I mean I look weak, there.

Dan: It's pain, not weakness. I think it's just right, is that.

Paul: Do you?

Dan: It's spot on. It *should* hurt.

Paul (*frustrated*): It fucking well does. (*He moves away.*)

Dan (*deflated*): I know.

Paul (*low*): Fuck.

DAN moves to PAUL and puts an arm around his shoulder.

Paul: What?

Dan: Nothing. I was just, you know, trying to help. Whatever.

Paul: You don't think we should do another take?

Dan: I don't think you're ready right now. Even if there could be a better one.

PAUL shakes his head. He allows DAN to hug him.

Dan: This is right, Paul. You know that. What we're doing – it's right. It's going to be a cracking bit of work. But we need every bit of it. Rachel's research, your words, the sequencer pictures, my secretions, the lot. Don't start getting second thoughts on me now.

Paul: Sure. No second thoughts. It's just like vertigo, now and then.

Dan: That's because it's good. And because it's good, it's dangerous.

DAN kisses PAUL's cheek. A look between them. HAWA continues working. The light lingers on her a while, before fading to black.

Scene 10

Actor: Weeks later.

DAN and PAUL in the studio. They are huddled around a lap-top/ projector hook-up. PAUL gives up and leaves DAN to it. He turns his attention to a booklet. He opens and reads it. DAN is absorbed in the various, as yet abortive, attempts to project an image. RACHEL is facing HAWA. Evening.

Rachel: You take some finding.

Hawa: Rachel Unsworth. You want to give me more dollars, so I never need to work again. I can sit in the shade all the day and watch the water in the lake turn blue then black.

Rachel: I thought you did that anyway. What's the job?

Hawa: I was in the flower-fields... cutting and sorting. I prefer the bean sheds: it's hard, and boring, but you don't get sick from the sprays they use.

Rachel: You've been ill?

Hawa: Nothing. So you want to take my blood again?

Rachel: No. I'm done with that for the moment. I just came to see how you are. Solomon wouldn't tell me anything about why you'd gone... or where you might be.

Paul: Weird.

Dan: What?

Rachel: Anyway it's gone really well. The research. Thanks to you. They sent me back to Nairobi because Solomon said he'd tracked down more people who are showing signs of immunity. So we had to check them out. To see if they're doing that in the same way as you. It turns out you were right about Solomon – he sort of tried it on with me. The arrogance! And he'd made up the newest results, I think. Messing us about.

Hawa: He's a man.

Rachel: Well he's a disappointed man, now.

Hawa: Is your medicine ready?

Rachel: Oh, that's a long way off. All we're doing is finding out if there's a way forward. Someone else – well, lots of people – will be involved in finding a way to turn it into a treatment.

Dan: Well? What?

Paul: They'll try to put your gene into a virus. That's how they administer it.

Dan: A virus?

Paul: A non-harmful one.

Dan: Like an inoculation?

Rachel: So this is your mother's house?

Hawa: I bought it for her.

Rachel: She's lovely. She smiles like you. (*Pause.*) You can see the lake from here. It's so beautiful.

HAWA sits and indicates for RACHEL to join her. They look out over the lake.

Dan: There.

Hawa: It's good to sit in the evening sun.

The screen floods in a glorious blue. A series of images dissolve on it: a sequence of stills of a sequencer graph, labelled 'Dan', zooming ever closer to the cluster of peaks and troughs, picked out in red and black, which represent the precious mutation. PAUL and DAN cross the space so that they are standing, silhouetted against the screen with its quietly shifting images.

Paul: Well done, Dan.

Dan: This should be Hawa now.

An identical-looking sequence labelled 'Hawa' runs, super-imposed on 'Dan'. The correlation is pretty exact.

Hawa: I'll take your medicine when it's ready.

Rachel: You won't need it. It only contains what you have already, the thing that's stopping you getting sick.

Hawa (*pause*): And are you famous, now?

Rachel: Me? God, no. Not really. Graham – he's my boss – he'll be very famous if this all works out. I might be a bit better known among scientists. I don't know if that's something to be pleased about or not.

Hawa: When are you going back to London?

Rachel: In a couple of weeks.

Hawa: I want to see London. You could take me there.

They sit, smiling at one another – mutually bemused.

Dan: There'll be that ambient soundtrack we discussed here.

Paul: I get it.

The screen darkens to black and the white legend 'Useless' appears.

Rachel: You're right. I could. Have you got a passport?

Hawa: No. But it's only a matter of knowing who to bribe.

RACHEL spots damage on HAWA's upper arm.

Rachel: What's this?

Silence. They look at one another. A darker tone.

Paul: I got a call today.

DAN looks at PAUL. Silence.

Hawa: It's nothing... nothing important.

Dan (*ecstatic; aghast*): Not from...

Paul (*building*): Only the very man himself.

Dan (*shouting*): You're kidding. You bastard, why didn't you tell me?

They hug, laughing, before the screen. They fall silent again and glance once more at the screen, which shows a sequence of dissolved stills of the different stages of development of a human embryo.

Hawa: I will meet the artist... Paul.

Rachel: Yes. No avoiding that, I'm afraid. Your arms, Hawa. These are lesions, I think.

Hawa: Doctor Rachel.

Rachel: You're... unwell.

Hawa: I forgot my fear... then fevers started... and I began sleeping too long. That's all.

Rachel: When did you last have your blood tested?

Hawa: There's no need. I'd like to see London.

Rachel: There are treatments, Hawa... drugs that suppress...

Hawa: But tell me, Rachel, what happened to your baby?

Silence.

Rachel: I'm taking you with me.

A final stilled image of the fully-formed baby in the womb. No other source of light. It fades.

Scene 11

Actor/Screen: Weeks later.

DAN and PAUL, at Dan's. PAUL is holding a mobile. DAN, the proofs for the 'Useless' catalogue.

Dan: What do you mean they're on the way over?

Paul: It was Rachel.

Dan: They're coming here, now? She's got Hawa with her?

Paul: She's always got Hawa with her.

Dan: We need to finish this.

Paul (*correcting*): We need to get it out of the way.

Dan: But it *has* to go back to the printer's tomorrow. Those photos in the centre are crap. The colour's nothing like. Some ham-fisted kid on work-experience, by the look of it. Why did we use these people? I told you I could do it better myself, didn't I.

Paul: Maybe we can meet really early, tomorrow.

Dan: What are you talking about? Tomorrow we're with...

Paul: Fuck! I'd forgotten about him.

Dan: So let's get on with it.

Paul: Rachel's about to walk right *in* here.

Dan: What the fuck are you talking about?

Paul: They took the underground – that's what I've been telling you. She was phoning from the station.

Dan: WHAT?

Paul: From the station.

Dan: And you didn't even try to put her off? Christ, we can do without your guilt trips just now.

Paul: What guilt trip?

Dan: You feel so bad about what we're doing that you *want* to be discovered. You *want* her to find out that we've nicked her research, and that you've spilled your guts about her; about the abortion. So, if she finds out now, she can get an injunction or something.

Paul: I'm not guilty of anything.

Dan (*defiant – a test*): We stole files off her computer.

Paul: She left it lying around – that's not theft.

Dan: It's work she's been doing for months; it's work in progress.

Paul (*tense*): It's not illegal.

Dan (*fierce*): She might just think it a tad immoral, that's all.

Paul: And what *she* did *isn't*, I suppose? All this qualms-shit, Dan. We're making art.

Dan: Good.

Paul: Everything's in place. And it looks fucking brilliant. It *is* fucking brilliant.

Dan: And we shouldn't we give her the heads up? If there's one bit of you thinking that, there's still time.

Paul: If you tell her anything we won't be doing any more work together.

Dan (*smiles*): Right. So phone her back and put her off. And we can finish making our work.

Paul: How can I? They're practically in the street by now.

Dan: You can still put her off. Tell her anything. Tell them to meet us at the pub, tell them the house is on fire... anything.

Silence. DAN gathers up the proofs and carefully slots them in a portfolio.

Dan: Oh, forget it. I'll stick this lot upstairs. I'll finish proof-reading the text tonight. You'll have to leave it to me.

Paul: What?

DAN makes for an exit and turns.

Dan: You do trust me, don't you?

Paul: Yeah... sure. Proof-reading.

Dan (*almost bitter*): It's a detail thing.

DAN goes. PAUL phones.

Paul: Hey it's me. I was just thinking we could go to the pub. We'll meet you there... I dunno, that one – the Eagle... what's that? We could eat there... at the Eagle, yeah. (*He makes for the exit.*)

Paul (*low*): Oh... sure.

PAUL exits and shortly returns with HAWA and RACHEL – they are carrying bags of food.

Paul: That was quick.

Rachel: We're hungry.

Paul: Hi, Hawa.

Rachel: I'll take that, shall I? (*She takes the mobile from his hand, ends the call and hands it back to him.*)

Rachel: We'll try talking, shall we... normally... unless you're kinky that way with phones?

Paul: Right. Me? God yes, mobile sex – it's the best.

Rachel: Where's Dan?

Paul: Upstairs, sorting something out.

Rachel: Come in properly, Hawa. Here. Paul, take the bags will you?

Paul: Sure. Christ, what've you got in here?

Rachel: Hawa's been pining for *real food*. African food. So we went to the market – it's amazing. I thought we could all eat together. You've been working all day. You need a break, don't you? So we decided to surprise you with a feast. Where's the kitchen?

Paul: Through there.

Rachel: We'll get on with it, then.

Paul: Just like that?

RACHEL goes to PAUL and kisses him.

Rachel: Just like this. God, I really fancy you.

Paul (*warmer*): Really?

Rachel: Oh, yes.

DAN re-enters the space.

Rachel: But I'm starving. I need feeding... right now.

Dan: Hi.

Rachel: Dan. We're cooking. It's going to be brilliant. We're having... shit I've forgotten again...

Hawa: We don't have to cook.

Rachel: We *do*. They'll love it. Take us to the kitchen, Dan.

Dan: It's through there.

Rachel: What's it called, Hawa – the dish we're making?

RACHEL grabs HAWA by the hand and leads her through to the kitchen.

Hawa (*as exiting*): Sukuma Wiki. But we don't have to make it.

Paul: Oh, aye?

Dan (*tight, to PAUL*): Nice one.

Rachel (*off*): God, it's amazing in here, Dan.

Dan: They're going to cook in Lawrence's kitchen.

Paul: Are you alright?

Dan: *I* don't even cook in Lawrence's kitchen.

RACHEL reappears.

Rachel: Great kitchen, Dan.

Dan: I know.

Rachel: You've even got an electron microscope in the corner.

Dan: Cappuccino maker.

Rachel: But you've got no pots and pans. What's that about?

Paul: Shit. I didn't think, Dan...

Dan: It's okay.

Rachel: Didn't think what?

Paul: They're all put away. Dan made a piece of work out of them, remember?

Dan: It's okay.

Rachel: Oh, that video thing.

Dan: It's fine. It was never supposed to be permanent.

HAWA enters with a large copper pan, which she is unwrapping.

Hawa: We can make the dough in this, I think.

DAN shrugs. He takes the muslin cloth from her and ties it gently around her, as an apron.

Dan: Of course you can. Use whatever you like. There now, Hawa, one chef ready to go.

Paul: I want one of those.

Dan: Help yourself.

Rachel (*faux-astonished*): You want an apron! You're going to do the cooking?

Paul: Hawa and me. Aren't we Hawa? Don't look so scared. I'll do just as I'm told. Tell me about this making dough-business – that sounds right up my street does that.

HAWA smiles at last.

Hawa: Bring the bags. We'll need the maize flour. We have to make ugali.

They go. RACHEL and DAN stand a moment.

Rachel: Look, the kitchen... Lawrence's stuff...

Dan: It's fine.

Rachel: Like, obviously not.

Dan: It's time I let go of all that. I know. Fuck it. I need a drink.

Rachel: Good. Let's get shit-faced. (*She produces two bottles of beer from a bag.*) Nice and cold – we got them from the fridge.

DAN takes the top off and hands the bottle back to her.

Rachel: This is an amazing place.

Dan: You've not been here before, I forgot.

Rachel: Do I get the tour?

Dan: Lawrence's – all of it.

Rachel: What did he do?

Dan: You'll take the piss.

Rachel: Cheers.

Dan: Cheers.

They both drink.

Dan: International banker.

Rachel: Right.

Dan: He left it to me – the house. His people made a fuss about it. But the will was rock solid – he was very careful about stuff like that.

Rachel: Don't you get lonely here, on your own?

Dan: No.

Rachel: So how come you and Paul started working here, all of a sudden?

Dan: That's different – it's work. And it's only for a while. It made sense for this project. There's more room. Paul suggested it, actually. One day when we were knee-deep at your place.

Rachel: And everything's ready?

Dan: For the opening? No way. There's still loads to do.

Rachel: How's the catalogue? Let's see it.

Dan: No. (*Pause, then lighter.*) I mean, no chance, girl. You'll have to wait like everyone else.

Rachel: I don't get Paul being all secretive. Usually he goes on and on about nothing else – what's the big deal?

Dan: You'll have to wait. I've just realised, I'm hungry.

Rachel: Good.

Dan: How long will it take, this stuff Hawa's making?

Rachel: Haven't a clue.

Dan: Is she okay?

Rachel: How do you mean?

Dan: She looks, I dunno, sick. She's always tired.

Rachel: It's not easy, is it. Everything's strange and new, still. She gets terrified on the underground. She just grabs my hand so tight. You know, like when the lights flicker out. And the noise kind of does her head in.

Dan: And everyone else there trying to look so fucking hard.

Rachel: Exactly. She had a bit of a romantic notion of it before she got here. My fault, I'm afraid.

Dan: How come?

Rachel: *We* met on the tube – Paul and me.

Dan: I know. (*Pause – covering.*) He told me once.

Rachel: She's going to the exhibition.

Dan: What?

Rachel: Adamant.

Dan: Right.

Rachel: Thought you'd be pleased. You worried what she'll make of it?

Dan: I'm worried what *everyone* will make of it.

Rachel: Relax. It'll be brilliant.

Dan (*pause*): Really beautiful, isn't she.

Rachel: Yes.

Dan: Paul wants to make photos of her.

Rachel: Does he? Why?

Dan: He said the other day. Would she let him?

Rachel: Probably – she never seems to object to anything. I kind of wish she would, sometimes.

Dan: Maybe she'd let us take some tonight.

Silence – both at a loss.

Rachel: Know what?

Dan: What?

Rachel: If I can't see the catalogue I want a look at your finger-painting book. The one you did with Lawrence. I'd love to see it... or is it totally private and personal and stuff?

Dan: It's personal, certainly. I've never thought about whether it was private.

Rachel: Forget it. It's fine. None of my business.

Dan: No. It's okay, really it is.

HAWA enters.

Rachel: Something wrong?

Hawa: Paul is doing everything, now.

Rachel: You shouldn't let him take over. He's terrible for that.

Dan: Too right.

Rachel: And it wouldn't be so bad if he had a clue what he was doing.

Dan: No comment.

Hawa: All he has to do is stir.

Dan: Want a beer?

HAWA shakes her head.

Rachel: You sure you're okay?

Hawa: I need some air, that's all.

RACHEL goes to her and puts her arms around her.

Dan: Hey, what's wrong? You aren't feeling well. Sit for a minute.

Hawa: I'm okay.

Dan: No, come on.

DAN clocks RACHEL.

Dan: You ought to see the doctor.

Rachel: It's okay. We've got it covered.

Hawa: Rachel looks after me.

Dan: I should bloody well think so. You're precious, you are.

HAWA looks away.

Dan: We used to spend hours out here.

Rachel: What's all this stuff growing in the pots?

Dan (*low*): Lawrence's herbs. I've done nothing to them, they should all be dead by rights. I'll get you some water.

Hawa: Thank you.

RACHEL sits beside HAWA, an arm around her, as DAN disappears inside.

Rachel: What is it? You feel faint or something?

HAWA smiles.

Hawa: It happens now and then. (*Pause.*) I just felt Kito – like when he was still in my womb, waiting to be born. He weighs so much. He weighs like a huge round stone in here. Kito still in my womb. The only time he had enough of everything. The only time there was enough of everything for him. The only time I could give him everything he needed. I wish he was still in here. (*She looks around at RACHEL.*)

Hawa: Well, you know. You know how it is when you lose your child.

DAN reappears, armed with a bottle of mineral water and the book. He opens the bottle and offers it to HAWA. The book he hands to RACHEL. She takes it and starts to flip through.

Rachel (*low*): Thanks, Dan.

Dan: Don't be daft. You let me see *your* work. Fair's fair.

Rachel: Not exactly the same is it? And it's your DNA, it's probably intellectual property rights or something.

Dan: I can smell burning – should I be able to smell burning?

Rachel: Paul's useless in the kitchen.

Dan: I'll go and rescue him.

Rachel: No. He usually screams if he gets really distressed. (*Of the book:*) Where was this?

Dan: Uh... New York.

Rachel (*softly*): *We* went, a few years ago. Paul just sort of kidnapped me and took me. I'd only known him a month. It was wonderful.

Dan: We had a great time there, too. Lawrence showing off his hometown.

Rachel: I didn't know.

Dan: Yeah, he was a Yank.

RACHEL turns another page. PAUL emerges up stage, resplendent in improvised muslin headscarf and apron. He's carrying a copper pan, prodding the contents dubiously with a wooden spoon.

Paul: I need a second opinion. The wooden spoon stands up in it indefinitely, so it's thick enough now, right?

Dan: What have you done to the pan?

Paul: Might be a bit, you know, singed at the bottom. Don't worry, I'll scour it.

Dan: You go near that with a Brillo and you're dead.

Hawa: Show me.

Paul: Here.

Hawa: Put a dish or a plate over the top. Turn it upside down and the dough will drop out, in one piece.

Paul: Take more than gravity, I think, to do that.

Dan: I was saying to Rachel, that you wanted to take pictures of Hawa.

Paul: You were, were you?

Hawa: You are going to draw a picture of me?

Paul: Would you like that?

HAWA smiles.

Rachel: You don't do drawing.

Paul: I could. I was thinking of taking some photos, just to start with.

Hawa: Photos.

Paul: Only if you agree.

Rachel: Not now, eh.

Hawa: No. It's fine. Take your photos.

Fade to black.

Scene 12

Actor/Screen: A week later.

On the screen, the 'Useless' footage runs as before, in scene 10. Final image of the unborn child appears – we can hear PAUL's voice, pre-recorded. His image dissolves in, over that of the baby. It is the filmed account he gave to camera in Scene 9.

Paul: Thing is... the thing is... I'm crap at everything, not just singing. Evolution says I'm crap – expendable – because I'm a man. She told me once that the point of the male, in evolutionary terms – which are the only ones which have any weight for her – that the point of the male had been to fertilize the ovum, and that now science has found ways of doing that without us. She said inception – that first impulse, the one which turns an egg into an embryo – can be achieved by introducing a small electrical charge. That's all we ever were, men, just a couple of volts, or something. Not even enough to turn over the starter motor of a family saloon, oh, no. Just about enough juice to change channels. That's it. So of course she aborted our baby. A bit of DNA from anyone she takes a fancy to, and she can zap herself one another day... when it suits her... when she's finished her beautiful work...

This footage loops as long as necessary – but at a low sound level from now on. A small, lit, space snaps on – rich colour. HAWA is standing in the light, staring intently and with amused wonder at an artwork. PAUL is just to one side of her, observing her. A further, small, lit space emerges elsewhere – rather dim tones. RACHEL is standing alone in the light. Aghast, she makes a slow circle. DAN stands, awkwardly, at the edge of this space, watching her.

Hawa: This is the picture? This is your picture of me?

Paul: It *is* you.

Hawa: Four coloured lines?

Paul: That's you.

Hawa: When did you make it?

Paul: We assembled it – Dan and me.

Hawa: Assembled?

Paul: We put it together. Out of your DNA readings.

Silence.

Paul: From the blood sample Rachel took – pumped through the DNA sequencer – turned into a picture.

Hawa: This is *Rachel's*...

Paul: No. It's *yours*. And we assembled it here... we gave it a meaning... here.

Silence.

Paul: That's the artist's job – to make meaning.

Hawa: What does it mean?

Paul: Different things to different viewers?

Hawa: What does it mean?

Silence. They look at one another.

Paul: Well, what does it mean to you?

Rachel (*softly*): Arseholes.

Hawa: Can you draw?

Rachel (*softly*): Total... complete arseholes.

RACHEL turns to DAN, who steps forward.

Dan: Look. I'm sorry, Rachel.

Paul: Of course I can draw.

Hawa: Four coloured lines that Rachel made. It's not a picture of me.

Paul: Then, that's what it means to you.

Hawa: Maybe.

Paul: Maybe that's all you mean to Rachel.

Rachel: This is my work. You've taken my work. You've been at my laptop, or something. And you've just...

Dan: Out of order... I know.

Hawa: You think that that's all I am to *her*. To Rachel.

PAUL smiles. HAWA turns to look at him again. A long, appraising look.

Dan: To start with we were just going to use the stuff about me.

Rachel: And that's why you changed your mind about providing DNA?

Dan: No. But it *is* mine after all ... I guess it wasn't supposed to go this far.

Rachel: What does that mean? It's not your fault? Your name's above the door, Dan. I haven't even got within a month of publishing any of this. Christ, Dan... *this* stuff is about Hawa.

Dan: I know. It's wrong.

Rachel: Wrong. You don't even begin to understand how wrong.

HAWA indicates another space.

Hawa: What's in here?

Paul: Some of Dan's DNA.

Hawa: A picture like this?

Paul: Go and look, if you like.

They cross to another space. HAWA again scrutinises items (out of our view?). She is amused/perplexed.

Rachel: Hawa's HIV-positive.

Dan: What?

Rachel: That's how wrong this is. It's not even accurate.

Dan: I didn't know.

Rachel: Of course you didn't know. It's a fucking contravention of freedom of information for you to know. I shouldn't have told you now. But... for fuck's sake. What else have you done?

Dan: So. We got it wrong. But that's sort of the point we're making, isn't it?

Rachel: The point?

Dan: That's the point of the whole 'Useless' thing.

Rachel: Our research is useless?

Hawa: Little glass tubes.

Paul: Capillaries... very thin...

HAWA peers, PAUL observes.

Dan: Well, it *is*.

Hawa: Dan's blood?

Paul (*pointing elsewhere*): No, *this* one's blood. That's excreta.

Rachel: In the opinion of two ill-informed, arrogant shits.

Dan: It *is* useless. Hawa's dying.

Rachel: Two little shits who publish hacked-up fragments of my work.

Dan: Hawa's dying.

Rachel: Before I've had a chance to verify, to test, the whole project could be stillborn.

Paul: This room was Dan's idea, mainly.

Hawa: Can Dan draw?

HAWA makes a methodical scrutiny. PAUL starts to enthuse.

Dan: There isn't going to be a gene therapy for AIDS.

Paul: Blood.

Rachel: You don't know that.

Paul: Shit.

Dan: There isn't.

Rachel: There wasn't one in time for *Lawrence*.

Dan: This isn't anything to do with Lawrence.

Rachel: But that doesn't mean we shouldn't try. That we shouldn't keep on trying. What about all the others?

Paul: Urine.

Rachel: Jesus, Dan. What else have you done?

We see her focus on the space with the screen we can see.

Hawa: And this is Dan's spit?

PAUL shakes his head. HAWA peers again; looks back at him, open mouthed.

Dan (*to RACHEL*): More of the same, really. More of the same.

Rachel: What's in here?

Dan (*low*): Going in there would be a bad idea, Rachel.

RACHEL goes into the space with the screen and stands facing it – absolute stillness in her now. HAWA starts laughing.

Hawa: You and Dan – too much time on your own... too much time on your own.... Where now?

Paul: It's up to you.

HAWA's focus turns to the screen we can see. He watches her move away from him and enter that space. The other lit areas darken now. The sound on the looped footage is brought up. HAWA and RACHEL are silhouetted against the image of PAUL speaking directly to camera. When the line about Rachel aborting the child comes around, HAWA's focus clearly turns to RACHEL. RACHEL becomes gradually aware of HAWA's presence and turns slowly to return her stare. DAN watches them from one side. We see him turn away and disappear into the darkness. PAUL is looking out at the audience. He is distressed. The sequence of images of the unborn child is running. RACHEL turns from HAWA, glances at an image and leaves the space, walking past PAUL as she does so, without acknowledging him. After a moment, PAUL follows her. HAWA remains, looking at the screen.

Fade to black.

Scene 13

Actor/Screen: Months later.

Paul and Rachel's flat. They are standing facing one another in the space – awkward. There is a holdall.

Rachel: I wasn't sure if you'd to be in.

Paul: I can go if you like. Leave you to it.

Rachel: No, no. It's fine.

Paul: Give you an hour, or something.

Rachel: I can't stay long.

Paul: Right. (*Pause.*) I reckon I found everything. All your stuff.

Rachel: Thanks for doing that.

Paul: I don't think there's anything else. But have a look around... obviously... be my guest.

Rachel: It's fine. There were just a few clothes I liked, that's all.

Paul: And some photos.

Rachel: Photos?

Paul: Some photos you took...

Rachel: I never took any photos.

Paul: Photos of me.

Rachel: Did I? I don't remember ever taking any. I remember *you* pointing cameras at *me* all the time.

Paul: In New York. Our hotel room.

Rachel: That's a long time ago.

Paul: You'd been asleep, on the bed. And I just wanted a shot of you sleeping. But you woke just as I was focussing. And you went ape-shit. You sat bolt upright. And you were naked and just so beautiful that I couldn't move. Then you shouted at me and got hold of my camera...

Rachel: We had a *fight*.

Paul: We were playing.

Rachel: We were play fighting. That's right.

Paul: I was trying to get the camera back.

Rachel: And I was taking shots.

Paul: You were taking shots. Firing them off.

Rachel: I didn't have a clue.

Paul: I know.

Rachel: I'm a useless photographer.

Paul (*pause*): You aren't actually.

Rachel: I remember the fight but I never saw the photos.

Paul: I know. I only developed the film the other day. It was in a bag full of them... you know how crap I am at labelling things. I went through them. Developed the lot. It took days. (*Pause.*) This one film. It was just a few more shots of Manhattan to start with and I'd almost stopped looking when I saw this one of me – all blurred with movement – but definitely me. Then I remembered it all. Instantly.

Rachel: You put them in my bag?

Paul: Just a contact sheet. I've got the negatives. If you want I'll blow some up for you.

Rachel: That'd be good.

Paul: I would've done it already, but I couldn't presume...

Rachel: Presume what?

Paul: That you'd want any photos of me. Rachel, I'm sorry.

Silence.

Paul: We did a crass thing... no, a callous thing. I was callous. I wanted to hurt you. I really wanted to hurt you – I wanted you to cry. That's the truth of it. I'm sorry.

Silence.

Paul: I keep reading about you, in the papers.

Rachel (*almost coy*): Don't.

Paul: I think it's great. You come over very... I dunno...

Rachel: Earnest, or something?

Paul: Impressive.

Rachel: I kind of hoped you wouldn't see any of the coverage. It felt exposing, to imagine you reading that stuff

– and it's never hard science is it, just broadsheets making out that they're taking it all seriously... and me trying to be sort of not too technical... not too cold.

Paul: You aren't cold.

Rachel: You didn't always think so.

Paul: I'm a useless prick. What do I know.

Rachel (*low*): Useless.

Silence.

Paul: It sort of worked out, though, didn't it. The publicity.

Rachel: There's certainly been a lot of interest. No development funding yet.

Paul: You'll get it. And it's going to work – a cure.

Rachel (*correcting*): A therapy. It's looking more hopeful... there may be something to field test soon.

Paul: Brilliant, then.

Rachel: It's good for everyone. Graham's over the moon – but it would kill him to actually admit it. He's pissed off that no one ever wants to interview him about it.

Paul: You're more media-friendly. I think that's the expression.

Rachel: Code for my tits.

Silence.

Rachel: How's Dan? He's scared shitless of me.

Paul: Yeah, he is.

Rachel: Is he here? Hiding in a cupboard somewhere? There's no need... I haven't got a problem with Dan.

Paul: He's in San Francisco this week.

Rachel: With the buyer?

Paul: Bud. You heard about him?

Rachel (*smiling*): Of course. I don't only read the papers when I'm in them.

Paul (*smiling*): But that's what they're for. (*Pause.*) Dan's supervising the installation over there. Silly money we're getting.

Rachel: I don't think so.

Paul: You what?

Rachel (*warm*): If the point is to make us question, to stop us in our tracks, to make us see ourselves somehow, to show us the state we're in, to make us trip over something that can't be explained away... then it's a great piece of work. Like a good bit of science.

Silence – eye contact.

Rachel: I think 'Useless' is probably the only really great thing you've ever done.

Paul: If I could undo it, I would.

Rachel: Well, you shouldn't. In fact shame on you. You've a job to do.

Paul: A public duty. Just like you.

Rachel: I won't ever wish it undone.

Paul: Are you and Graham together? None of my business, I know.

Rachel: No, it isn't.

Paul: So, are you?

Rachel: Yes.

Paul: I kind of thought you might be.

Rachel: I'm leaving the project now.

Paul: Get out of here!

Rachel: I can't work with him. It was always difficult and it's impossible now. So I'm moving on.

Paul: But it's about to be massive, surely.

Rachel: I've finished the bit that interested me. Anyway, I'm going on to something new.

Paul: So... what now?

Rachel: You think I'd tell *you* about it? And have you turn it into an arcade game for chin-stroking cappuccino drinkers or something?

Paul: Alright, I deserve that.

Rachel: And more.

Paul: I'm thinking about slicing off my genitals...

Rachel: Yeah, yeah, the old Van Gogh gag. Well don't. Not on my account. Anyway, that would be a shame. A waste.

Paul (*flat*): Really.

Eye contact.

Rachel (*still light*): He never mentions my freckle.

Paul: Graham?

Rachel: Stephen Hawking/Orlando Bloom! Who the fuck do you think!

Paul: Freckle One.

Rachel: Vanilla tasting.

Paul: That's you that freckle is. He's got to be a special kind of stupid not to be talking to you about Freckle One.

Rachel (*low*): I've missed you.

Paul: Hole in the head.

Rachel: I miss having sex with you.

Paul (*a decision*): I've been having sex with me for years – it's not that great.

Rachel (*pause*): There's something else.... No.

Paul: What?

Rachel: No. I'd better go.

Paul: Okay. Good to see you.

Rachel: Thanks for sorting out my stuff. (*She picks up the bag and turns to face him again.*)

Rachel: I *will* tell you about the new project, though... if you really want to know. I've been given the go-ahead to look into the effect of emotions on the production of certain proteins. Links to the immune system.

Paul (*at sea*): Wow.

Rachel: I'm leading it. I've got a team, a lab and everything.

Paul (*warm*): Brilliant.

Rachel: Fieldwork starts next week.

Paul: Kenya?

Rachel: Kenya. I'll look at those photos when I'm on the plane.

Paul: I like to think of you doing that. (*Pause.*) You'll give Hawa my love, won't you. You are visiting her, aren't you?

Rachel: Of course I am. I still need her blessing.

Paul: For what?

Silence.

Rachel: I'll see you around then. (*A brief kiss from her and she moves away, leaving him. She stops at the exit point.*)

Rachel: She called her baby Kito – it means 'precious'.

Paul (*low*): Every baby should be called that.

Rachel: Every baby *is* called that. (*Pause.*) Hawa couldn't understand why I had the termination.

Paul: Neither could I.

Rachel: Bollocks, Paul. You understood. You just didn't like the reason. Hawa couldn't understand... and I couldn't explain it to her. It didn't make any sense when I said it to her.

Paul: Because it was wrong.

Rachel (*tight*): I knew it.

Paul: What?

Rachel: You're still waiting, even now. You're still waiting for an apology from *me*. You're still waiting for me to prostrate myself before you.

Paul: I'm not...

Rachel: Well, you'll be waiting a long time for that, Paul. You still think that I terminated it just like that, just like – what was it? – 'changing channels'. You're still just as stupid and as insensitive and narcissistic, and just as... fucking grotesque and adolescent, Paul. We didn't have a baby. For a few weeks there was an embryo. That's all. It's not the same thing.

Paul: How is it not?

Rachel: Because having a baby is what I'm doing now.

Paul: You what?

Rachel: *That's* why I came to see you. I'm pregnant.

Silence.

Paul: Graham's?

Rachel: Of course Graham's. And Hawa will bless us. (*Pause.*)

You can say congratulations at this point, if you like.

Silence. She shrugs and goes.

Fade to black.

The Company

Krissi Bohn (Hawa)
Krissi trained at the Manchester Metropolitan School of Theatre, graduating in Summer 2004. Theatre productions whilst in training include: Bertha in *The Kitchen*; Moon in *Blood Wedding*; Chastity in *Moll Flanders*; Alithea in *The Country Wife*; Gemma in *Cigarettes and Chocolate*; Mrs Sullen in *The Beaux Strategem*; Anya in *The Cherry Orchard*; Lady Gloucester in *Henry VI*.

Krissi is delighted to be making her professional debut in her native town of Plymouth.

Jonathan Lisle (Paul)
Jon trained at LAMDA and the Anna Scher Theatre. His recent theatre credits include *Spinach & Chips* (New End Theatre); *Masks & Face* (Finborough Theatre); the Nigerian tour of *Things Fall Apart*. He has also been involved in the rehearsed readings of *Tamburlaine* and *The Rover* (The Old Vic & Young Vic respectively). Other theatre credits include *First Hand*; *Science Friction*; *Love Fifteen* and *Shepherd's Delight* (Riding Lights Theatre Company); *Comedy of Errors* and *King Lear* (Cambridge Shakespeare Company); *Aristocrats* (Runaway Theatre Company); *A Few Good Men* with the Synergy Theatre Project. Television and Film Credits include *The Story of Daniel* (International Films Ltd); *Fade to Red* (Tant Lay Productions); and ident spots on GMTV's *This Morning*.

John Morrissey (Dan)
John graduated from the Oxford School of Drama in 2003. Since graduating, theatre credits have included *Dance Hall Days* (Riverside Studios, London); *A Slight Ache* (606 Club, London); *Epsom Downs* (Cockpit Theatre, London); *Absent Father* (The Old Red Lion, London). Television

credits include *Crimewatch UK*. John has also appeared in commercials for Smirnoff Ice and Dockers Jeans.

Clare Wille (Rachel)
Clare trained at RADA. Her theatre work includes *Wuthering Heights* (no.1 tour); *Racing Demon* (Chichester Festival Theatre and Toronto); *Look Back in Anger* (London Classic Theatre). TV credits include *Doctors*; *Where the Heart Is*; *Life Begins*; *Heartbeat*; Jacqueline Wilson's *Girls in Love*.

Jeff Teare (Director)
Jeff has directed over 100 professional productions, most recently: *Turn Of The Screw* (the Wolsey, Ipswich); *Love and Other Ambiguities* (Greenwich); *Football* (Edinburgh Festival). He has also taught in drama schools; written and presented TV documentaries; and worked as an actor, musician, playwright, education consultant, and video maker. He is currently the consultant/practitioner on Theatre Royal Plymouth's 'Theatre of Science' Project. He was a founder member of Medium Fair Community Theatre Company for South and East Devon; Studio and TIE Director at Derby Playhouse Theatre; Associate Director at The Young Vic; Staff Director at Royal National Theatre; Associate Director (1986-95) at Theatre Royal, Stratford East; Artistic Director at Made in Wales (1995-2000).

Jane Linz Roberts (Designer)
Jane Linz Roberts has designed contemporary and classic work in the UK, USA, Canada, Romania, Ukraine, Germany and Australia, including: *Doctor Faustus* (National Theatre/Plymouth Theatre Royal); *The Railway Children* (Nottingham Playhouse/Oxford Playhouse); *The Silver Sword* (Nottingham Playhouse); *Listen to Your Parents* (Nottingham Playhouse/Theatre Centre); *Double Indemnity* (Theatr Clwyd); *The Whisper of Angels Wings* (Birmingham Rep); *Everything Must Go* (Lyric Hammersmith); *A Christmas Carol* (New Victoria,

Stoke); *House of America* (Fiction Factory/ Perth Festival, Australia); *Song from a Forgotten City* (Y Cymni/Donmar Warehouse/Royal Court/Bonner Biennale/Melbourne International Festival and Bulandra Theatre, Bucharest); *Translations* (Theatre on Podol, Kiev); *Cwm Glo* (Theatre Gwynedd/Bucharest); *Translations* (Theatre on Podol, Kiev); and – while Resident at the Sherman Theatre – *Macbeth*; *The Merchant of Venice*; *Midsummer Night's Dream*; *My Beautiful Laundrette*; *Under Milk Wood*; *Of Mice and Men*; *Everything Must Go*; and *The Lost Child*.

Thomas Hall (Video Designer)
Thomas is an artist and filmmaker. Artistically, he is interested in public intervention and empowerment with media technology. His artwork has toured nationally and internationally and uses new technologies (such as motion tracking and image matting) and large-scale projection sited within public spaces. His short films and music videos have been shown at numerous festivals and broadcast on national networks. Recent moving image projects for theatre have included *The Lion, The Witch and The Wardrobe* and *Captured Live*, for Leicester Haymarket Theatre. Future projects include music videos for Deep Water Recordings and a large public piece for the market square in Nottingham.

Bruno Poet (Lighting Designer)
Bruno has lit over 100 productions of theatre, opera and dance in the UK and Europe. Over the past year, his work has ranged from theatre shows in London and other cities – *Dumb Show* (Royal Court); *Don Juan* (Hammersmith Lyric; Manchester); *Volpone* (Royal Exchange, Bristol); *Alice in Wonderland* (the Old Vic and in Leeds); *The Lemon Princess* for the Caird Company (West Yorkshire Playhouse) – to his seventh consecutive season for Garsington Opera.

Rebecca Gould (Producer)

Rebecca is Associate Director at the Theatre Royal and an Education Associate at the National Theatre. She has recently produced *Football* by Lewis Davies for Made in Wales at the Edinburgh Festival. Directing work includes: *The Wonderful Life and Miserable Death of the Renowned Magician Doctor Faustus* and *Little Tempest* (National Theatre); *Romeo and Juliet* (English Shakespeare Company); *Venus* by Peter Morgan and *Gulp* by Roger Williams (Made in Wales); *The Jolly Folly of Polly the Scottish Trolley Dolly* and *Eggplant* by Greg Ashton and James Williams for The International Festival of Lilliput.

Theatre Royal Plymouth

The Theatre Royal Plymouth is one of the most successful regional producing and touring lyric theatres in the UK. The organisation consists of two, distinctive performance spaces: the Theatre Royal and the Drum Theatre, as well as TR2 – an award-winning theatre production and education centre.

The range of work presented and produced at the Theatre Royal is vast, making it one of the best attended regional producing theatres. National companies that make the Theatre Royal their home in the South West include Birmingham Royal Ballet, Glyndebourne, Welsh National Opera, and Rambert. In addition, we welcome major touring drama, musical and dance productions.

The Theatre Royal also produces or co-produces a number of drama and musical productions each year, many of which transfer to the West End or tour nationally. As part of an ongoing collaboration with the producer Thelma Holt, the Theatre Royal has also produced a series of Shakespeare productions which have been successful on national tour.

However, the Theatre Royal is only one auditorium. the Drum Theatre is a smaller, new-writing venue that welcomes and produces the most innovative and cutting edge new work in the UK. An exceptional venue in the South West, the Drum enjoys a national reputation for the highest quality, and as one of the most exciting centres for new writing, regularly producing with Frantic Assembly, The Bush, Paines Plough, Royal Court, Told By An Idiot, and Out of Joint.

The newest addition to the organisation is TR2 – our production and education centre. A truly unique facility in the UK, this state-of-the-art, award-winning building provides unrivalled production, wardrobe and rehearsal facilities which enable the theatre to continually produce work for both stages. But production is only one part of its existence. At TR2, the Arts Development and Education team provide an essential service to the local and regional community. As well as running youth and community theatre groups, the team also works with educational establishments throughout the South West on projects ranging from skills-based workshops to large-scale performance projects. The capacity of TR2 enables the theatre to run one of the biggest education and outreach programmes in a regional venue in the UK, and our objective is to continue to expand and develop this work.

The Theatre Royal Plymouth is a forward thinking and creative organisation which aims to be a cultural resource for its local community, the wider South West region, and for a national audience.